AMONG ~the~ LEAVES

A Collection of Outdoor Essays

GEORGE ROGERS

CORNERSTONE PRESS
Stevens Point

Published by Cornerstone Press
Department of English | University of Wisconsin-Stevens Point
2100 Main Street, Stevens Point, WI 54481-3897
(715) 346-4342

Direct comments to cornerstone@uwsp.edu
Visit our website at www.uwsp.edu/english/cornerstone

Copyright © 2012 George Rogers

All rights reserved.
No part of this book may be reproduced or transmitted in any form or by any other means (including electronic means, photocopying, recording, or any other information storage and retrieval system) without the written permission of the author.

Library of Congress Control Number: 2012951451

ISBN: 978-0-9846739-1-9

Printed in the United States of America
First Edition: November 2012

Printing, collating, and binding made possible by a generous contribution from:
Worzalla Publishing
3535 Jefferson Street
Stevens Point, WI 54481-0307

This book has been printed on paper containing 30% post consumer recycled material.

Photography by George Rogers unless otherwise indicated under the photograph.
Cover and book design by Sara Rebers.

All profits from the sale of this book will go to the Environment Mission Fund of the Community Foundation of Central Wisconsin.

Table of Contents

Foreword by Bill Berry ix

Introduction 1

The Land 3
The 22 Apostles 4
THE State Park 8
The Mead Battleground 12
Buena Vista 16
Dewey Marsh 19
Treasure Island 22
A Land History 24
Isle Royale 27
Tropical Camping 29
The Green Circle 32
Room to Roam 34

People 37
Louis and Ike 38
The Princeton Man 40
The Gunsmith 43
The Odd Couple 45
DuBay 48
Mary Had It Right 50
A Link With the Past 53
Hornberg 55
Les Was More 57

Table of Contents

Mammals   59
Deer Revival   60
Jackass Rabbit   63
Deer Don't Stand Still   65
The Water Walker   67
Bounty Hunters   69
The Big, Not-So-Bad, Wolf   73
Return of the Natives   76
Mammal Count   80
Frequent Roadkill   82

Fish Life   85
Musky Luck   86
Walleyes   88
The Fish Book   90
The Poetic Justice   93
Rough Fish   95
To Set a Record, Lower Your Sights   98
The Fly Tackle Capital   100
Don't Like 'em? Then Eat 'em   103
Fish Potpourri   105
Unglamorous, but ...   107

Bird Life   109
Egg Salad   110
The Missing Bird   112
Symbol of Peace?   115
The Prairie Chicken   117
A Comeback Story   120
Bluebirds   122

Rivers   125
Our Namesake River   126
Dam Facts   129
Little Plover   132
Tomorrow   135
Harry's Dam   138

Mill Creek	*140*
Mill Ponds	*142*
A Cleaner River	*144*

Adventure — 147
Flambeau	*148*
Up Fuji	*151*
A Perilous Trip	*154*

Plants — 157
The Right Pine	*158*
Not Just a Crazy Weed	*160*
Forest Primeval	*162*
The Juniper-Bird Link	*165*
Big Trees	*167*
Wisconsin Cactus	*169*
The Scrub Pine	*171*
Poison Plants	*173*
The Grass Killer	*175*
Prolific Pollinator	*177*

Odds and Ends — 179
The Wisconsin Dog	*180*
Butterflies	*182*
Clamming	*184*
Creepy, Crawly Critters	*186*
Snoop and Scoop	*189*
Homemade Fakes	*191*
Lake or Dry Land?	*193*
Mound Builders	*195*
Changing Rules	*197*
A Hard Water Business	*199*
Fracking Sand	*201*

Conclusion — 203

Selected Bibliography — 205

Foreword

This gift from George Rogers is meaningful in so many ways.
First, it is an excellent collection of essays about the outdoors and environment that will enlighten and entertain for years to come. You don't have to be from Central Wisconsin to enjoy *Among the Leaves.* Many of its essays have universal appeal and timeless messages. Some have appeared in column form, in either *The Portage County Gazette* or *The Stevens Point Journal.* Others are gleaned from George's many outdoors experiences and from his extensive study of the topics as a reporter, editor, adventurer, and voracious reader.

The collection also has historic value to Central Wisconsin and beyond. It captures the birth and growth of a better understanding about the natural world around us, and how we humans have a huge impact on nature, for better or worse. George is succinct in describing his goal for the book: "Mostly, I hope it alerts people to the need to protect our environment, including air, water, and soil. We, as a people, haven't been doing that very well, though we seem to be getting a little better."

For those of us who know George, the book is special because he is a man of few words, someone who leaves you wishing for more.

Foreword

Now, for the first time, a collection of essays by George Rogers is being offered to readers, many who have come to relish every sentence he constructs. The man tells a story like no one else.

The book includes several sections full of facts, anecdotes, and observations. It also names names. Those who've lived here a while will recognize references to the likes of Dan Trainer, George Becker, and Fred and Fran Hamerstrom. George knew them all. Readers who aren't familiar with those names and others captured in this book will learn something about people who left important legacies.

Among the Leaves is only a small part of George's larger body of material. As a journalist, he has been chronicling life in central Wisconsin and beyond for eight decades. He continues to pursue the journalist's trade to this day. Want proof? Look at his breast pocket. More than likely, it will contain a notepad and pen. George once described taking notes as an incurable habit. We are all better for his indulgence.

It would be remiss to not point out some of George's other gifts to the community. He co-chaired a committee that raised funds for the downtown Stevens Point county library. He was president of the committee that planned and implemented the multi-use Green Circle nature trail enjoyed by thousands every year. He and his wife Jeanette have devoted themselves to many other community causes, but they're not braggers, so let's leave it there.

Thanks to Cornerstone Press for sharing this gift from a remarkable man.

—*Bill Berry*

Introduction

This isn't one of those "me and Joe went fishin'" books. If that's what you're looking for, try *Field & Stream* magazine.

I'm writing for hunters and fishers, but also for birders, bikers, hikers, and just plain nature lovers, who also have a claim on the outdoors. Most of what I've written is about things, people, and places in the middle of Wisconsin because that's what I know best.

The book has no plot. It contains chapters unrelated except that they're about the outdoors. I'm dedicating it to my wife, Jeanette, and our son and daughter, Jim and Jane. To them, I'll add Bill Berry, who talked me into writing it and also critiqued it.

By way of background, I've lived all my life in Stevens Point, Wisconsin, except for a couple of years in the Army. I hunt and I fish, not expertly but with enthusiasm. However, an ankle problem has ruined me for trout fishing and grouse hunting.

I was editor of the *Stevens Point Journal*, and later a founder of and a writer for the *Portage County Gazette*, a Stevens Point weekly newspaper. My duties at both papers included writing an outdoor column.

For this, I blame Bill Berry. I had just become editor of the Journal and he had succeeded me as news editor.

One day, he came into the office and said, "This newspaper needs an outdoor column." Since I had written a lot of outdoor stuff over the years and had only one real deadline a day, I decided to give it a try.

In my first column, I said this might be the first in an irregular series, meaning I might soon run out of material, and instead of appearing weekly, it might show up every two weeks, or three, and then not at all. It turned out that there was plenty of material and I've written well over a thousand columns of varying quality, and they're the source of much of the material for this book.

I've also tapped into the expertise of people at the Wisconsin Department of Natural Resources and the University of Wisconsin-Stevens Point College of Natural Resources. They're too numerous to mention individually, but they have my heartfelt thanks.

—*George Rogers*

Trout streams on the Buena Vista Marsh, once winding creeks, are now almost as straight as sidewalks.

THE LAND

The 22 Apostles

I wouldn't mind visiting Cat Island again, but not to hunt deer. I did it once and the experience was great, but the deer were scarce.

Cat Island is in the Apostles, a 22-island archipelago in Lake Superior off the Bayfield Peninsula. Twenty-one of the islands and a strip of mainland constitute a national lakeshore, part of the National Park System. All the islands are in it except Madeline.

Half of Cat Island was owned by Hiram Anderson of Stevens Point before the creation of the national lakeshore, and a group of us once hunted there. A commercial fisherman named Harvey Nourse took us out, getting us to shore by running his boat up on a sand spit since there was no dock.

The island was uninhabited, but on the shore was a cottage, sort of. I won't insult Hi Anderson's memory by calling it a shack, but it lacked modern conveniences like plumbing, electricity, wall-to-wall carpeting, air-conditioning, a patio, and central heat. Still, it provided shelter, though it wasn't a place to spend the winter.

After hauling our gear up to the building, we went exploring and met some guys who were camping and hunting on the island. They had a buck hanging from a tree limb, and one of them said, "Well, we got THE deer," implying that it was the only deer on Cat island. He was wrong, but not by much.

The next two days, we hunted. The island had been logged long before and the big timber was gone, but a lot of smaller stuff had grown up and it provided good cover for any deer that might be there. And there were a few, darned few. One of our party got a shot at one but missed. I saw the east end of one going west, but it disappeared into a thicket before I could get off a shot. And that was it, as far as hunting was concerned. In the evening, we played poker by lantern light.

It got stormy when we were on the island, and Lake Superior can get rough and dangerous. A lot bigger craft than Harvey Nourse's have gone to the bottom of Gitchee Gumee, and Harvey told us he wouldn't have come out for us if the weather hadn't improved. I don't remember whether we had enough food to last us a couple more days. We sure wouldn't have eaten venison.

But the storm abated and Harvey came for us and brought us safely back to Bayfield. It's been said many times that there's more to hunting and fishing than shooting game and catching fish, and our Cat Island expedition proved it. Just being on an uninhabited island was an experience, something that doesn't happen much these days.

I understand Hi's shack is no more, but has been replaced by the Park Service with a more modern cottage you can rent. The waiting line to reserve it is long, I believe. Some people still want to get away from civilization for a few days.

Another of the Apostles with a Stevens Point connection is Outer Island, which, as you might guess, is the one farthest from the mainland. Lullabye Furniture bought it in 1936, all except a lighthouse. They wanted the hardwood timber on the island for its factory in Stevens Point and its veneer mill in Butternut.

According to a 1936 story in the *Stevens Point Journal*, the island had 40 million to 50 million board feet of timber on it, much of it old-growth hardwood and hemlock. The big timber hadn't been logged because the island is far from the mainland and it would have been hard to raft the logs in, as hardwood doesn't float as well as pine.

To log it, Lullabye flew lumberjacks back and forth, using an air strip on the island. The problem of getting the logs to the mainland was solved after World War II when Lullabye bought a surplus LCT (landing craft, tank), a 100-foot-plus vessel that had been used in amphibious landings in the European theater.

The LCT survives, possibly the last one of its kind. It is docked at Bayfield and I believe it's used for dredging and marine construction. Its name? The *Outer Island*, of course. In 2004, it was the subject of a program on public television.

When Lullabye owned Outer Island, local people went there to hunt deer, which possibly were more plentiful than they were on Cat Island. While it lasted, the Outer Island logging operation was a good one for the company. "I wish I could do it over again," said Lullabye's Vic Bukolt.

Lullabye didn't skin all the trees off, as some of the old-time lumbermen did, but for one reason or another, the logging operation became unprofitable and Lullabye sold Outer Island. The island went through a couple of changes in ownership, then became government property when the national lakeshore was established in 1970. Federal interest in the islands was stimulated in 1963 when President John F. Kennedy flew over the Apostles, probably at the urging of Sen. Gaylord Nelson, and was impressed.

Outer Island was the scene of an unusual wildlife experiment in the 1960s. The Wisconsin Conservation Department, now the Department of Natural Resources, got the idea that a huge European grouse, the capercaillie, might make a good addition to the state's wildlife inventory and that Outer Island would be a fine place to test the theory. It imported 30 capercaillies from Finland and released them onto the island.

Male capercaillies can weigh up to 15 pounds, so if the transplant had succeeded and the state had a five-capercaillie daily bag limit, you might have needed a wheelbarrow to haul your kill out of the woods. But they didn't make it. Vic Bukolt theorized that Outer Island's eagle population had something to do with it.

The Land

The history of the Apostle Islands goes back thousands of years, to Indian times. Logging, brownstone quarrying, commercial fishing, and even farming are part of the story. People lived on some of them, but today only one has a resident population. That's Madeline, the biggest of the Apostles. It has a village on it, La Pointe, with some 300 residents, a number that mushrooms during the summer tourist season.

The first European to reach the Apostles was French explorer Etienne Brule, who got there about the time the Pilgrims were landing at Plymouth Rock. Later, a Catholic mission was established. The French named the archipelago. If they were thinking of honoring the 12 Apostles, it was a serious miscount.

Madeline Island was named for Madeline Cadotte, daughter of Chief White Crane and wife of Michael Cadotte, a French fur trader.

You can get to Madeline Island by air—it has a 3,000-foot paved landing strip. Or you can take a car ferry from Bayfield. In winter, there's an ice road between the mainland and the island, and when the ferry isn't running and the ice is unsafe, there's a windsled ferry—a flat-bottomed boat with an airplane propeller on the back.

On the other islands are campgrounds. No ferries exist to them, but you can use your own boat or hire someone to take you out. And an excursion boat can take you on a tour of the Apostles. Many people kayak around the islands, which have interesting sea caves along their shores.

THE State Park

Long ago, Wisconsin had a state park bigger than any existing today. It mysteriously vanished. I wanted to learn more about it but ran into a dead end, so I wrote to *Wisconsin Natural Resources* magazine, published by the Department of Natural Resources (DNR), suggesting this would make a good article.

For a long time I heard nothing, but finally I got a letter from the editor. Good idea, he said. *YOU* write the story.

Nuts to that, I thought. I wouldn't know where to start. Any historical material that still existed, I believed, was probably buried in the archives of some state agency in Madison, and I had no desire to spend days down there digging it out.

Then I got to thinking: If I didn't write the article, no one else would, and I'd never find out about the park. So I contacted the State Historical Society and asked if they had any material. The society's response was: what park are you talking about? The state has lots of parks. I couldn't get it across that this was *THE* state park, the only one in existence at that time, the 1870s.

Finally, I made contact with a woman in the DNR state headquarters who gave me some helpful leads.

What I learned was that the park covered, or would have covered,

760 square miles on the border of Upper Michigan. It would have encompassed most of Vilas County and part of Iron County. Hundreds of unspoiled lakes, many miles of stream, and a great expanse of old-growth timber were within its boundaries. If it still existed, it would be looked on as the eastern version of Yellowstone National Park, minus geysers, bison, and grizzly bears.

The park was created in 1878 by an act of the Legislature on a motion by William Baker of Monroe, a member of the Assembly. It's not clear what motivated him. One theory is that he was just trying to slow down the sale of state-owned timberland.

Whatever his reason, the idea was good, but flawed. The state didn't have title to the whole 760 square miles and in fact owned only about 10 percent of it. Presumably the state could have bought the rest, but the temper of the times was against it. This was the logging era, and the lumber barons who carried a lot of weight in state politics wouldn't have been happy to see a vast expanse of timberland turned into a "playground."

Besides, people had a different attitude toward nature back then. Wilderness wasn't prized the way it is now. The public for the most part welcomed logging as a way to prepare the north for agriculture. Farming, in fact, did follow but was mostly a flop for reasons of soil, climate, and distance from markets.

The park idea was not without its fans. A Madison newspaper, the *Democrat*, called the proposed park, "one of the wildest and most beautiful spots in the lake region. The whole tract is studded with scores of charming lakes which constitute the source of streams running toward every point in the compass. The park has never been thoroughly explored and few settlers have undertaken to make a permanent residence, but it abounds with fish and game, and if preserved in its natural perfection will be one of the finest bequests the present could possibly hand down to coming generations. It needs no improvements over what nature has done for it."

Absolutely true, but the wisdom was ignored. Additional land wasn't acquired, and in 1897, the state sold its holdings for an average of $8 an acre.

Had the park become a reality, there's no assurance that the pristine woodland would have escaped fire, windstorm, forest succession, or timber theft (old-time lumbermen were famous for their poor eyesight when it came to property lines). Still, it's nice to imagine what could have been.

Lakes in the park would have included Fence, Trout, Big and Little Arbor Vitae, Big and Little St. Germain, Plum, Star, Presque Isle, Crawling Stone, and hundreds of others. (Vilas County alone has 555 named and 771 unnamed lakes with a total acreage of about 145 square miles, according to the Wisconsin Lakes booklet, published by the DNR.)

Most likely the park, had it survived, would resemble the wild Sylvania tract just across the state line in Upper Michigan, only bigger.

Today, a lot of state and county forestland exists within the boundaries of the proposed park. The timber is nice, but I'm sure it doesn't compare with what was there in the 1870s. The lakes are still there, but the great majority are developed—in fact, often over-developed.

An effort is being made to reconstruct the park, or something like it, on a smaller scale in the form of the Wild Rivers Legacy Forest, a 101-square-mile area in Northern Wisconsin that's being protected, mainly through the efforts of the Department of Natural Resources and the Nature Conservancy. It won't, for the most part, become an old-growth forest. In fact, logging will be permitted in most of it under a management plan, helping support the local economy. But the forest will be protected against rampant development and will be open to the public.

I wrote an article about the park-that-never-was, and *Wisconsin Natural Resources* magazine printed it in its December 1995 issue. I don't consider it a great article. Had I had the time and inclination to more thoroughly research the park, I might have been able to learn more about the reasons for creating it and why our almost-Yellowstone didn't survive.

The article didn't make me rich, since *Wisconsin Natural Resources* magazine didn't pay me. I was told to take a tax deduction. But at least I satisfied my curiosity about the origins and death of the park.

If there's a lesson to be learned from the fate of *THE* State Park, it's this: Hang onto what we have in the way of outdoor resources. Development schemes may look good today, but what are their effects on coming generations?

The Mead Battleground

The George W. Mead State Wildlife Area in Central Wisconsin was the victim of abuse. It has recovered.

Today, it is 30,000-plus acres of restored wetlands and forests at the junction of Marathon, Portage, and Wood Counties. It's home to a great assemblage of wildlife and a place where school children are taught about the environment.

Mead was a larder for the Indian tribes that inhabited it for thousands of years. It was the site of the half-legendary Battle of Smoky Hill in about 1755, when Wisconsin was part of New France.

Smoky Hill is a bump of land in an otherwise flat part of Mead. Accounts of the battle were passed down over the years and recorded in Malcolm Rosholt's book, *Pioneers of the Pinery*.

A historical marker at the site says the hill was a Chippewa (Ojibwe) encampment. The story goes that one day a group of the Chippewas went down the Little Eau Pleine River, which runs through Mead, to tap maple trees. In their absence, some Winnebagos (Ho-Chunks) moved in.

Rosholt wrote that the Chippewas didn't try to oust them, either because they were outnumbered or because the Ho-Chunks were holding their wives and children hostage. So they asked the French at Green Bay for help.

The Land

The French came and brought muskets and a couple of small cannons. Some of the French helped the Chippewas drive the Winnebagos from the hill, pushing them eastward where other French were waiting with the cannons, inflicting heavy casualties. There's no written record of the battle, but John Moore, a University of Wisconsin-Stevens Point archeologist, said it's possible something about the French involvement is buried in archives in Quebec or Paris. Moore also said there was a rumor that the French left a cannon behind, but it hasn't been found.

After white settlers came, they hunted there just as the Indians did. Alex Wallace, an old-time Stevens Point resident, recalled in 1959 that in 1888, when he was 14 years old, he and his father were in a party of hunters who spent the month of October camping on Rice Lake in what is now the Mead Area. They got there by canoe and skiff, and Wallace said he repeated that October hunt for 14 years. There were no bag limits, and he said it was not uncommon for a hunter to shoot 10 ducks or more a day. Rabbits and grouse were abundant on the high ground and Rice Lake was "lousy with pickerel," which we now call northern pike.

In those days, people had the idea that wetlands were worthless unless farmed, so early in the 20th century, dredges went to work, straightening the winding Little Eau Pleine River and excavating ditches to move water out of the valley.

Like many other drainage projects, it was a failure, except possibly for the promoters who sold land to farmers. Wetland soils often look better than they really are. Frequently, they have peat soils, which have an unfortunate tendency to catch fire. Also, lowlands can be frost pockets, sometimes every month of the year.

So agriculture didn't work and much of the land went tax-delinquent. Consolidated Water Power & Paper Co. (later Consolidated Papers) bought up thousands of acres in preparation for the creation of a reservoir by the Wisconsin Valley Improvement Co., a coalition of power companies.

It was to be formed by a 2¾ mile long dam on the Little Eau

Pleine and was to be called the Mead Reservoir in honor of George W. Mead, Consolidated's president. It wouldn't generate hydroelectricity itself but would hold back water that would be released into the Wisconsin River during times of low flow, increasing power production at dams from DuBay all the way down to Prairie du Sac.

The reservoir was to be huge—18 miles long and 7 miles wide, with a surface area of about 27,500 acres when full. But when drawn down to keep the turbines running at power plants on the Wisconsin River, it would have been nearly empty, leaving much of the reservoir bed a mud flat.

Not everyone was thrilled. People still farming in the valley of the Little Eau Pleine didn't care to be displaced, and those not directly flooded out were concerned that the roads they used would be under water.

Most vociferous of all were conservationists, because the Little Eau Pleine Valley was still a wildlife haven despite the abuse it had taken from the marsh drainers. A few people thought the promised economic benefits outweighed the damage, but not people like Les Woerpel of Stevens Point, a telephone company employee and co-founder with Dick Hemp of what became the Wisconsin Wildlife Federation. He objected loudly and did his best to block the project.

The reservoir also had some silent skeptics, including Stanton Mead, son of George W. Mead and his successor as president of Consolidated. Times and economics were changing, electricity consumption was increasing dramatically, and he realized the demand couldn't be met by hydropower.

Still, plans for the reservoir proceeded for a time and permission to create it was granted by the Wisconsin Public Service Commission, then the agency in charge of such things. But in 1959, Consolidated called it off and offered to give the 20,000 acres it owned to the state for conservation purposes. It was an act that served as a precedent for other corporations faced with a choice between protection of the environment and business-as-usual.

The state accepted the gift and the Conservation Department put John Berkhahn in charge. His initial challenge was to undo the damage done decades earlier by the marsh drainers. When Berkhahn died, he was succeeded by Tom Meier, who continued his work and expanded it.

Mead's scenery is not spectacular, though duck and deer hunters and wildlife watchers might disagree. But its mixed habitat is great for wildlife, and it is managed for both game and non-game species. It is a land of diversity, with deer, bear, wolves, furbearers, and other mammals. And it is inhabited by or visited by a couple-hundred bird species.

Hunters, birders, hikers, and nature lovers are heavy users of Mead, which also serves as an educational institution. On its grounds stand the Mead Education and Visitor Center, an earth-friendly building constructed without public money.

The funds came from Wausau Homes, who donated the core of the building. Many other sources also contributed donations, including a public fund drive coordinated by Kent Hall, a retired University of Wisconsin-Stevens Point biology professor.

A great supporter has been the Mead Witter Foundation of Wisconsin Rapids, whose funds originated with the Mead family and Consolidated Papers.

The Mead Area has a full-time educator who works with the thousands of students who visit the place every year. Tom Meier, who retired in 2011 after 30 years as Mead's manager, considered environmental education not only a top priority for the wildlife area, but a necessity.

Buena Vista

The Buena Vista Marsh—wetland or prairie? Some of both. About a hundred square miles in the middle of Wisconsin, it was mostly a tamarack swamp before it was drained for agriculture with mixed results. Its troubled history includes Kentucky bluegrass, cattle, prairie chickens, trout streams, an extraordinary couple from the East Coast, and an Illinois university.

It has a Spanish name but no Spanish-speaking people were around when it was so designated. Apparently it was named, directly or indirectly, after a battle in the Mexican War, fought about the time white settlers arrived.

People farmed around the edges but agriculture didn't really take hold until Bradley Polytechnic Institute of Peoria, Illinois, now Bradley University, bought it in the early 20th century. Why did an institution of higher learning want to own a swamp? To make money. Bradley Poly had an endowment fund and used it to buy an Indiana wetland. It was drained and sold to farmers, resulting in a nice profit. So Bradley decided to do a reprise in mid-Wisconsin.

Ditches were dredged, trout streams that ran through the marsh were straightened, the water table was lowered, and the marsh came to look much like a prairie.

The Land

The land was then put up for sale to farmers. It may have worked out all right for Bradley, but it was a tough go for those who bought the land. Frosty summers, an agricultural depression that preceded the Great Depression of the 1930s, drainage assessments, and peat soils that sometimes caught fire and burned for months were some of the troubles the settlers faced.

The University of Wisconsin set up an experimental farm at Coddington, an unincorporated village, to show how to make agriculture work on the marsh. Coddington? It's probably the closest thing to an urban area on the marsh, sitting on a piece of high ground. It once had a post office and was a stop on the P-Line, a branch of the Soo Line Railroad that ran from Stevens Point to Portage and was discontinued after World War II.

Coddington came close to being discontinued, too. Writing in the late 1950s, local historian Malcolm Rosholt said Coddington had "failed the test of time," and in a few years might be unrecognizable, "as the only evidence of a village in 1958 was one abandoned store and a number of foundations for buildings long overgrown with weeds." But since then, the community has undergone a small renaissance.

Among the things the marsh can grow very well is grass, and Kentucky bluegrass at one point was an important crop, grown for its seed. But that ended when it became cheaper to import it from Europe. Bluegrass, it seems, isn't native to Kentucky or anywhere else in the United States. Northern Europe is where it originated.

Grass is good for cattle, so ranching took hold in the marsh. That was accompanied for a time by rustling, just like the Old West. Then came irrigated agriculture and cranberry growing.

Fish and wildlife? The marsh has both. In Colorado some years ago, I asked a man if he'd ever fished for trout in a drainage ditch. I think he thought I was demented, but then I told him about the ditches on the Buena Vista Marsh, some of which were once streams and have good trout populations.

You can find some unusual birds on the marsh, including snowy owls, which come down from the arctic in winter when lemmings are scarce. Evidently the marsh resembles the tundra.

The signature wildlife species on the marsh is the prairie chicken, a grouse found all over Wisconsin after the northern forest was logged and burned, but now confined to just a few areas, notably Buena Vista.

Dewey Marsh

Forest fires are far better controlled than they once were, but under certain conditions, they still run wild. In 1976, the Dewey Marsh State Wildlife Area and the land around it experienced a fire that ran for miles, damaged woodlands, and smoldered all winter in peat soil. But it harmed no buildings because there weren't any in its path.

The marsh lies in the town of Dewey, on the northern edge of Portage County. It was named for Admiral George Dewey, victor in the Battle of Manila Bay in the Spanish-American War.

Dewey was the last town created in Portage County, carved out of two other towns in 1898, and its western boundary is the Wisconsin River. In his county history, Malcolm Rosholt wrote that the river banks are "littered with Indian arrowheads and forgotten graves, rusty oxen shoes, abandoned mill sites, and old tote roads running to the logging camps farther back."

Logging and sawmills haven't disappeared from Dewey, but still it's a much changed place since 1898. The big marsh, however, is still there and still wild.

The core of the wildlife area was bought by the state in 1973. The initial purchase was 3,200 acres, and in 2012, the state owned about 6,000 acres out of a goal of 7,823.

When it became state-owned, some hunters thought it had the makings of another Mead Wildlife Area, with lots of waterfowl. It didn't. The Dewey Marsh has plenty of wetlands (along with high ground), but the quantity and quality of the water isn't conducive to duck and goose production.

However, Dewey is an asset in terms of other wildlife, and is heavily used by hunters for deer and small game, as well as by trappers, wildlife watchers, and hikers. It's one of the stops on the Great Wisconsin Birding and Nature Trail, which lists its signature species as the northern harrier, ruffed grouse, and the grasshopper, vesper, and savannah sparrows. During the fall migration, you may see small flocks of short-eared owls, and in winter, look for pileated woodpeckers. Red and white-winged crossbills are in the conifer swamps.

The property lies in the Hay Meadow Creek and Little Eau Claire River watersheds. The streams are sluggish and highly acidic, and neither has much potential for fishing—mainly bullheads and minnows. Dewey's strong point is forest wildlife, not waterfowl or fishing.

The area, six miles north of Stevens Point, is mostly flat and not very scenic if your idea of natural beauty is mountains, tall timber, and waterfalls. But a 1.5 square mile state natural area is within Dewey. It's an undisturbed northern sedge meadow, which is scientifically significant.

A few bumps of high ground in Admiral Dewey's marsh are identified on U.S. Geological Survey maps, oddly enough, as the Philippine Islands.

The 1976 fire damaged much of Dewey's forested land, and a master plan drawn up in 1982 said it had "a tremendous impact on wildlife species." The impact was beneficial for creatures that like open space, including prairie chickens and sharp-tailed grouse. But the trees regrew and this habitat largely vanished. However, Dewey continues to have good habitat for deer, ruffed grouse, and other forest and marshland animals.

It's not easy to get lost in Central Wisconsin, but I succeeded in doing it in a forested part of Dewey. I was grouse hunting on a completely overcast day. I headed back to my car from the edge of the marsh and found myself going in circles. Finally, by choosing a tree in front of me and walking to it, and then taking aim at another tree, and so on, I got to where I wanted to go.

The edges of the wildlife area were farmed long ago and attempts were made to drain the marsh. But agriculture was generally a failure, and the state put the marsh on its acquisition list in 1961. Herb Schneider, a conservation warden here in Portage County at the time, was a leading advocate of the purchase. So was Forest Ranger Bill Peterson, who in 1976 was in charge of the team that fought the big marsh fire.

The Dewey Town Board initially opposed state ownership, citing the loss of tax base and the fears of farmers that geese would cause crop damage. The state's payment in lieu of taxes is greater now than it was then, and high goose numbers never materialized.

The Department of Natural Resources task force that drew up the master plan for the marsh was headed by Bruce Gruthoff, a wildlife manager. The plan called for the property to remain largely roadless. The walk-in concept would meet opposition at first, Gruthoff said, "but a few years later, people wouldn't want to see it any other way. Nobody wants to be run down by a motorcycle when grouse hunting." Nor while bird watching or berry picking.

He also said, "20 years from now, my kids and other kids are going to be able to walk out into more than 7,000 acres of wild land. It wouldn't be that way without public ownership."

Treasure Island

Whoever talked Edward and Lavina Field into buying that farm was a world-class salesman. He clinched the deal not by what he said but by what he didn't say. He didn't tell Ed and Lavina the farm was on an island, and though he mentioned it was near Plover, he didn't say the Wisconsin River was between the farm and the village.

The Fields made the best of it. They named it Treasure Island, and in some respects it was a treasure. The soil was good and a bridge spanned the narrow gap between the island and the shore. However, the bridge was on the side of the river opposite from Plover, and ice and high water took it out one spring. When it was replaced, the same thing happened. After that, the family got to the mainland by boat or, in winter, over the ice.

Treasure Island wasn't always an island. Old maps show it attached to the west bank, but the Wisconsin River cut a new channel and separated it from the mainland.

The island is big and the farm, though it covered 120 acres, encompassed just part of it. The couple grew fodder there for a herd of Jersey cows, which give rich milk. Their daughter, Jan Hughes, who later wrote a history of Treasure Island called *Crossing a*

River, said "that was before fat had a bad name."

The milk was loaded on a truck and ferried to shore. Those were the days of the milkman, and it was distributed to Stevens Point homes under the name "Treasure Island Dairy."

Sometimes the cows grazed on a small nearby island, wading or swimming to get there. "That was the cows' idea," Mrs. Hughes wrote. "Greener pastures. It was really a lush little island, and on a hot day they liked to go in the water." It was her job to take a rowboat and round them up.

Treasure Island is among a cluster of islands where the Wisconsin River makes a sharp bend to the west. Wildlife was abundant, said Mrs. Hughes, and the river even had sturgeon, big ones that sometimes leaped from the water and landed with a splash. Sturgeon were later extirpated from the river above Wisconsin Dells, probably by pollution and dams that blocked spawning runs, but the Department of Natural Resources is reintroducing them.

Mrs. Hughes wrote that she was home-schooled until the seventh grade. After that, she rowed a boat to the Plover shore and walked a mile to school. In winter, she boarded with a Plover family.

The Field family farmed on the island from 1907 to 1937. After they left, the buildings were being vandalized so the family had them burned.

In the 1930s, Portage County applied for the creation of a Civilian Conservation Corps camp in the area, and one of the projects proposed for the CCC boys was the development of a park on four islands in the vicinity of Treasure Island, but apparently not including Treasure Island itself. Bridges for pedestrians and saddle horses would have connected the islands to each other and the mainland. But nothing came of it.

Now the island is uninhabited, except for wildlife. Some people call it Field's Island, but others still call it Treasure Island.

A Land History

There's a story behind every piece of land. Some of it is in the records at the register of deeds' office and some is locked up in memory, or simply forgotten.

The story behind 40 acres I own north of Stevens Point isn't dramatic. No battles were fought there, and no one struck oil. But it has a tale to tell about the passage of time and the changes that come with it.

According to my abstract of title, the first owner of record, in 1856, was a man named James Howley. I don't know where he came from, why he acquired the land, or what happened to him after he left. And I don't know for sure what the land was like when he got title from the federal government, which had obtained it through a treaty with the Menominee Tribe.

The field notes of the men who made the original government land survey might tell me what was growing there, but I haven't checked. It's not near water, so I'm sure it was never the site of an Indian village.

The land was unglaciated but nevertheless was affected by the great ice sheet that stopped five miles to the east. When it melted, the outwash deposited a layer of sand on my land. Because of that,

The Land

I'm guessing the tree cover was jack pine and scrub oak, or possibly it was a savanna, a mixture of oak and prairie.

Fire and wind may have periodically changed the vegetation. What little topsoil was there eroded once the land was cleared for agriculture.

Howley owned it only briefly. The next owner was Silas Walsworth. He was a lumber raftsman and co-operator of the Star Saloon in Stevens Point. Walsworth may have been the one who cleared it. Or maybe he was too busy tending bar and rafting lumber down the Wisconsin River, and a later owner did it.

It was farmed, but because the soil was infertile and susceptible to drought it must have been difficult. Farming was abandoned years before I bought it, and the open part (about 33 acres out of the 40), was being invaded by jack pine and black cherry. In a couple of places, wind erosion had scoured the soil down to bare mineral sand where nothing grew, not even sand burrs. The vegetation on the other seven acres was scrub oak and jack pine.

I saw an old map that showed a building of some kind on the land, but it had been razed or moved off before I bought it. Not even a trace of a foundation remained, so maybe the building had just been resting on logs.

The struggles of the people who tried to farm it are an untold story, and possibly a sad one. It must have taken a heroic effort to make a living there, and it's not surprising that agriculture eventually ended. Clearly this land wouldn't grow decent crops except in the wettest of summers. Would it be productive farmland today if irrigated? Maybe, but there's no irrigated land nearby, a hint that the ground water source is inadequate.

But trees did well on the poor soil. I ordered 40,000 red pine from the Department of Natural Resources and we planted them—"we" being a neighbor with a tractor pulling the tree planter, two college kids, and myself. We didn't work an eight-hour day and we didn't work from sunrise to sunset (about 14 hours at that time of the year). We worked from first light until dark and even after dark, dodging around scattered jack pines.

Although it was somewhat dry the year I planted, tree survival was good. I'd guess 90%, maybe better.

Is a pine plantation a real forest? Does nature plant trees in rows, evenly spaced, all of one species? No, but the trees have made the land better than it was. I've logged it several times, taking off the equivalent of about 1,900 cords of pulpwood, cabin logs, and saw logs. It isn't a gold mine but it paid for itself, thanks to a law, adopted by the state in 1927 and later amended, that imposes a significant tax only when trees are cut. Otherwise I'd have been taxed out of the tree business long ago and forced to subdivide it.

There was a lot of satisfaction in watching the trees grow and the land heal, and in spite of the logging, many tall pines are left. Before the most recent logging, I asked a DNR forester, Paul Lochner, for advice on replanting. Do nothing for a while, he suggested, wait and see what happens.

What happened was that pines are reproducing naturally—some of them red pine but mostly white pine, the seed coming from a few whites just off the edge of the property. The land is slowly beginning to look like a real forest.

No state forester was based nearby when I planted the trees, so I relied on advice from the county agriculture agent and from other people who had planted trees. A forester might have advised me to mix another tree species in with the red pines, probably white pines. Now I'm getting the white pines anyway, gratis.

My pine plantation isn't great wildlife habitat, but I think it never was. Still, I've seen deer there, along with turkeys, ruffed grouse and songbirds, even a scarlet tanager. The most unusual animal I ever saw there was a jackrabbit, a species that may no longer exist in Wisconsin. That was just before I planted the red pines.

Urban sprawl now surrounds my land, but I'd like to see it remain in trees. I regard this as its best and highest use, though certainly not as profitable as selling it for residential lots.

Isle Royale

I've been on Isle Royale, a national park in Lake Superior, just once. If you're going there to experience the nightlife, forget it. The principal carousers are wolves, and they're in trouble. But if you're looking for a place to get away from it all, it's a good choice.

The 209 square mile island has no year-round human inhabitants and it's the scene of a long-term study on the relationship between wolves and moose, predators and prey.

Isle Royale is closer to Canada than to the rest of the United States, and I think Ben Franklin was responsible for drawing the boundary line that put it in this country.

Bill and Jackie Hoppen and my wife Jeanette and I took a ferry to the island from Houghton, Michigan. You can also catch a ferry from Copper Harbor, Michigan, and Grand Portage, Minnesota. There's seaplane service, too, from Houghton. And if you're really adventurous, you can take your own boat, keeping in mind that Lake Superior is a big, treacherous body of water.

On the island, you can stay at Rock Harbor Lodge or in housekeeping cottages. Or you can camp out among the wolves.

What's to do? You can hike around in an unspoiled landscape, looking for wildlife. We saw moose but no wolves. But maybe the wolves saw us. They're secretive and don't bother people.

Neither animal has been on Isle Royale forever. Moose arrived early in the 20th century and multiplied, destroying much of the vegetation. They apparently swam to the island. Lake Superior is frigid but moose are almost impervious to cold. Some think people brought them there. Wolves arrived in the late 1940s, probably crossing on an ice bridge from Canada, something that rarely forms.

The wolves reduced the number of moose, providing a lesson in the balance of nature. They preyed mostly on moose calves and old, decrepit animals, since a bull moose in its prime can put up an effective defense.

Isle Royale's predator-prey relationship was never in perfect balance, with the number of both animals fluctuating. Generally it worked, but in time became really threatened. The wolf population dwindled and as of 2012 it appeared the animals could disappear from Isle Royale. The problem may be inbreeding—they're descended from a very few individuals.

If the wolves go, what next? More could be brought in, but the general policy of the National Park Service is to let nature take its course.

At one time, the Isle Royale wolves were the only ones remaining in the lower 48 states, other than those in Northern Minnesota. Now, of course, they've recovered in other states, notably Wisconsin.

Would I recommend a visit to Isle Royale? Sure. For us it was a good experience. If you plan to stay in the lodge or in cabins, make reservations. Same with the ferry.

Tropical Camping

I'm no globetrotter. My foreign travel has been limited, but one trip was especially memorable.

In 1994, our son Jim and I tagged along with students, a couple of faculty members, and a few other adults on a between-semesters field trip to Costa Rica. It was under the auspices of the University of Wisconsin-Stevens Point's College of Natural Resources and was educational for the students. And for us.

We stayed in a few modern places and also camped in pup tents. It was no hardship. Costa Rica is in the tropics so we didn't freeze, and we weren't there during the rainy season.

Costa Rica is a small, democratic, and peaceable country with a strong environmental ethic. It had an attempted revolution in 1950, after which Costa Rica abolished its army. There's a colony in the Monteverde cloud forest that was founded in 1951 by pacifist American Quakers after the Costa Rican army was eliminated.

While we were down there, a presidential election was going on. I don't speak Spanish so I don't know this for sure, but I think the campaigning was more civilized than it has been lately in this country.

Costa Rica has frontage on both the Atlantic and Pacific Oceans, as well as mountains, volcanoes, rain forests, cloud forests and dry tropical forests. It also has wildlife, including monkeys, jaguars, iguanas, coatis (raccoon relatives), crocodiles, and three-toed sloths. We spotted no jaguars—they're scarce and secretive—but we saw birds up the kazoo. The Mead Wildlife Area in mid-Wisconsin is a birding hot-spot and about 200 species have been seen there. Costa Rica has 650 species, more than all 48 contiguous American states combined. Some of the Costa Rican birds, like the oriole, come up here to nest.

The most spectacular Costa Rican bird is the male resplendent quetzal. It has gorgeous colors and an impossibly long tail.

We were in a cloud forest in Costa Rica where the hummingbirds were in a virtual holding pattern around feeders. This area, maybe the size of a typical Wisconsin county, has 30 hummingbird species. Not counting a rare stray, Wisconsin has one, the ruby-throat.

Costa Rica has four monkey species. One of them, the howler monkey, has a roar that would scare you if you didn't know what it was.

We camped along the Pacific coast on what must be one of the world's most beautiful beaches, Naranjo. It's totally undeveloped and in a national park.

A lot of the country's best environmental features are in parks, and will stay protected if they can resist the temptation of short-term gain. We have people who would sell Yosemite to make a buck.

No real road led to our camping site at Naranjo, so we walked seven miles to get there. At the beach, olive ridley sea turtles come in to nest. If their eggs aren't stolen by predators, they hatch and the little turtles immediately head for the sea, but some are picked off on the beach by vultures and frigate birds.

Besides unusual wildlife, Costa Rica has some spectacular plants. We saw a tree fern that must have been 40 feet tall. And then there's the cannonball tree, named for the huge, hard, and heavy fruit it produces. The theory is that giant mammals used to eat the fruit and disperse the seeds. The big mammals are gone now, and the tree has a hard time reproducing. I don't know what those fruits weigh, but I wouldn't advise camping under a cannonball tree.

The Land

In the rainforest, where we had no rain and mosquitoes were absent, we saw a long line of leaf-cutter ants, each carrying a piece of foliage. They were taking it back to their nest to grow fungus on it, which they eat.

At Naranjo Beach, the temperature must have been 90 degrees or better. When we got back to Wisconsin, we were in for a shock. The temperature dropped to 30 below zero.

The Green Circle

It was John Jury's idea when he headed the Stevens Point Parks & Recreation Commission. What about a hiking, biking, cross-country skiing trail around the community?

Others picked up on it and the Green Circle was born. It's 26 miles long, with spurs, and goes through parks and other public lands.

The initial planning was done by a highly informal, self-appointed, public-private committee that met weekly at Al's Diner. The members had breakfast, talked about a lot of irrelevant things and somehow laid the groundwork for the Green Circle. Despite the lack of organization, things got done, and now a more formal group is in charge.

There's public money in it, but also a lot of private funds. The community's enthusiasm for the trail has been a big help in fund raising.

Roy Menzel, one of the early members of the committee, wrote a book called *Home Town on the River* and donated the proceeds to the project. This went to pay for a master trail plan drawn up by Dave Aplin. Access problems have prevented Aplin's plan from being followed down to the last inch, but it remains the basic blueprint.

Menzel also submitted a list of possible names for the trail to the committee, which quickly decided on Green Circle, aptly named because it goes through a lot of greenery. And, of course, it circles the community. It's mostly off-road, much of it going along the Wisconsin and Plover Rivers, where the scenery is much as it was when logs and lumber rafts floated down.

The trail goes through Stevens Point and village of Whiting parks, the University of Wisconsin-Stevens Point's Schmeeckle Reserve, and other public lands. It also goes through private property with permission of the owners.

From the Green Circle, a branch goes south to Plover, where it connects with the Tomorrow River State Trail.

Dan Trainer and Bill Werner, early co-chairmen of the Green Circle Committee, said the trail would be an attraction for visitors but was mostly for people living here. And that's the way it has worked out. People do come from out of town to walk the trail, enjoy the scenery, and observe the abundant wildlife, but the thousands of people who live within a few minutes of the Green Circle are the biggest users.

Room to Roam

There's a lot of public conservation land in Wisconsin—about 6.3 million acres owned by federal, state, and county governments. That's about 18% of the state's land area. Is that too much?

In Texas, 95% or more of the land is privately owned. If you're a hunter or a fisher, give this some thought before moving to Texas. If you hunt deer in Wisconsin and can't find someone who will let you on his property, you can go to the Chequamegon-Nicolet National Forest, any of numerous state wildlife areas, or a county forest.

In Texas, you'll almost certainly have to pay a private landowner for the privilege of hunting on his property, and most likely you'll pay through the nose. That's right, Texas, the land of broad skies, open space, and many no-trespassing signs.

Some of the public land in Wisconsin is a result of foresight, like the Knowles-Nelson Stewardship program, which has bought many thousands of acres. Some is the result of hard times and bad economic decisions, which caused a lot of pain but wound up doing some good. The national forests and the Horicon and Necedah Wildlife Areas are made up, in large part, of farms that failed because of poor soil and hard times.

The Wisconsin counties with the most public land are in the

north, with its national forest, but many other counties have substantial acreages. In Wisconsin, county forests total about 2.4 million acres or almost 3,700 square miles, about as much as the Chequamegon-Nicolet. Douglas County alone has more than 425 square miles.

It adds up to a lot of land open to hunters and fishers without charge. Of course you'll need a hunting and/or fishing license, but you don't even need that if you only want to watch birds, look at the scenery, or just walk around.

If you still think 18% is too much land in public ownership, take a look at the state of Nevada, where 85% is government owned. And you'll find many fewer trees and a lot less water there than in Wisconsin.

Photo courtesy of UW-Stevens Point Archives
Dr. Daniel Trainer, "The Princeton Man"

PEOPLE

Louis and Ike

George Meyer, later secretary of the state Department of Natural Resources, once gave a talk in Stevens Point. Chippewa Indian spearfishing on Northern Wisconsin lakes was a burning issue then, and Meyer was questioned about it.

A federal court had ruled that the spearing was allowed because of treaties in the 1800s between the tribe and the United States government, in which the Chippewas had given up their land but retained certain hunting, fishing, and gathering rights. The rights still existed, the court said, and the specific terms should be negotiated between the tribe and the state. Meyer was one of Wisconsin's negotiators.

At the meeting where Meyer spoke, a man asked how come the Chippewas were allowed to drink in taverns. Wasn't that forbidden by the treaties?

Meyer proceeded to tell a story about Louis St. Germaine and General Dwight Eisenhower. After World War II, Eisenhower came to Northern Wisconsin to fish muskies, and St. Germaine, a Chippewa, was designated to guide him. Ike was said to be a pretty good fisherman and St. Germaine was a good guide, so they probably were successful.

At the end of a day of fishing, they left the water and headed back toward wherever they'd come from and Eisenhower suggested they stop for a drink. "You go in," St. Germaine said, "and I'll stay outside." How come? Eisenhower asked. St. Germaine explained that the treaty provision didn't allow Chippewas in bars.

The fishing guide thought the rule was discriminatory and so did the general. So when Eisenhower became president, Meyer said, he had the provision erased from the treaty.

I've never fished much with guides, probably a mistake because you can learn a lot from someone who fishes for a living. But once, when I was a kid, my dad hired St. Germaine. I'm not sure which lake we fished, maybe Squirrel, and I don't remember what we caught. But I do recall that St. Germaine was an interesting talker.

And I remember the shore lunch. In those days, guides not only showed you where the fish were, they fixed you a meal at noon.

We pulled up on shore and got the fire started and St. Germaine asked my father, "How do you want the potatoes fixed?"

"French-fried," my dad told him. He was kidding. You don't cook French fries over a wood fire on a lakeshore. But we had French fries.

Not having fished with a guide for a long time, I don't know if they still fix shore lunches or if they take their customers to McDonald's. Some of them do other things, like manufacturing fishing lures, giving speeches at meetings of fishing clubs, and even writing books. Some of the guides from the distant past could hardly read or write. But they knew where the fish were.

The Princeton Man

Dan Trainer sometimes referred to himself as a Princeton man. Was he really a graduate of that prestigious Ivy League institution? Not exactly. He meant he'd grown up in Princeton, Wisconsin, a small town in the south-central part of the state.

Dan had plenty of other things to brag about if he'd wanted to. He was an authentic authority on wildlife diseases, he served on the state Natural Resources Board, and he was dean for many years of the College of Natural Resources at the University of Wisconsin-Stevens Point.

At UW-Stevens Point, he took over a good program and made it the best. It had been started in the 1940s by Fred Schmeeckle, who saw a need for conservation education in the state's grade schools and high schools. The intent of Schmeeckle's program was to train people to teach conservation, and it worked.

A residence hall at UW-Stevens Point once had Schmeeckle's name on it but they took it off because they had something better to remember him by. It's the Schmeeckle Reserve, a 275-acre natural area on the north campus with a lake, trails, and a surprisingly large assortment of wildlife. It also has a visitor center that holds, among other things, the Wisconsin Conservation Hall of Fame, of which Fred is a member. So is Dan Trainer.

People

The conservation education program expanded and became the College of Natural Resources. Much of the growth came after Trainer was named dean in 1971. The college now has programs in forestry, wildlife, fisheries, soils, law enforcement, and more. And they're excellent programs. Once, at a meeting in Madison, I met a forester and asked him if he was a graduate of UW-Stevens Point. No, he said, he'd graduated from UW-Madison, "but I *wish* I'd graduated from Stevens Point."

Dan was no armchair naturalist. He was a great outdoorsman. Maybe it was genetic, as his father was a well-known conservation warden.

I'd be willing to bet Dan shot more deer than any other Wisconsin hunter in modern times. Hardly a season went by that he didn't get a buck. And as dean of the College of Natural Resources, he used to take students to the Welder Wildlife Refuge near Sinton, Texas, during semester breaks, and he continued his wildlife disease work there on deer. This involved necropsies, and to do a necropsy, you have to have dead deer. Dan made them dead with a rifle.

Could someone who killed all those animals be a wildlife lover? He could, in the case of Dan Trainer and others, like Frederick and Frances Hamerstrom. Those wildlife researchers from Plainfield were hunter-wildlife lovers too.

The Natural Resources Board on which Dan served is the governing body of the state Department of Natural Resources. He had great respect for people in the DNR and on its board but was no rubber stamp. When it came time to choose a new department secretary, he voted against the one favored by the majority. He had nothing against the man but thought the secretary should come from outside the agency to instill new thinking.

In fall, Dan and I used to canoe down the Plover River, hunting ducks. I think he enjoyed the river as much as he did the hunting. One fall, Dan told me he was passing up the canoe trip because his balance was no longer good. Then he was diagnosed with Parkinson's Disease. Later, I ran into him and he said, "I've got good news and

41

I've got bad news. The good news is, I don't have Parkinson's. The bad news is, I've got something worse."

What he had was multiple symptom atrophy, a rare and always fatal disease which took his life in 2007.

The natural resources building at UW-Stevens Point is named in his honor. Among his more enduring legacies are the 5,000 or more former students who studied at the College of Natural Resources during his time as dean. They're involved in natural resources management around the world.

Another legacy of Dan's is the state's Stewardship Program, which funds the preservation of Wisconsin's outdoor resources. He was on the committee that drew up the Stewardship Plan, and I'm sure his ideas helped make it happen.

The Gunsmith

If they'd had hunter safety courses in the 1800s, Jim Lee might not have limped. As it was, he shot himself as a boy and the effects lingered, but it didn't sour him on guns. He continued to tinker with them.

James Paris Lee was born in Scotland and as a child moved with his family to Canada, where the hunting accident took place. His father was a jeweler and watchmaker and Lee learned the trade from him. Shortly before the Civil War, he came to Wisconsin and set up a business in Stevens Point, a little lumbering town that had just been incorporated as a city.

The Pinery, a local weekly newspaper, wrote on March 23, 1860, that "Mr. Lee, we understand, comes amongst us as a genius—enjoying the reputation of being the inventor of the celebrated one hundred year clock—it being the closest thing to perpetual motion."

When he wasn't fixing clocks, he was doing other things, and he developed an extract of hemlock bark used in tanning leather. He made it at a mill on the Plover River somewhere above Stevens Point, but the mill burned. Maybe that's what persuaded him to concentrate on firearms.

At the start of the Civil War, soldiers on both sides were armed with muzzle-loaders. Inventors like Lee started working on breech-loaders, and he came up with a carbine that he sold to the government. It wasn't practical to make it in Stevens Point, which wasn't even on a railroad, so he moved to Milwaukee and manufactured it there. The Union army claimed defects in the rifles and Lee sued and got a partial settlement, but by that time, the war was ending.

He went east, worked for the Remington arms manufacturers in New York State and then struck out on his own, still developing rifles. Lee had little luck peddling them to the American military. He did sell a rifle to the Navy, but this wasn't a mass market as sailors have a limited need for small arms. Although, maybe the Marines, being part of the Navy, got the weapons.

Lee had better luck overseas, selling the British a rifle that became known as the Lee-Enfield. It was the British Army's standard infantry weapon through World War I, World War II, and the Korean War.

Before the carnage of World War I decimated it, Britain had a small but highly-skilled professional army whose members were crack shots. In *A World Undone*, a history of World War I, author G.J. Meyer wrote that British infantrymen armed with Lee-Enfields had been trained to hit a target 15 times a minute at a range of 300 yards. "Most could do better than that," Meyer wrote.

When German soldiers first encountered British troops in France, Meyer said, they met gunfire so devastating they thought they'd run into machine guns. Actually, they were Lee-Enfields.

Lee died in 1904. There's a historical marker honoring him in Wallaceburg, Ontario, east of Detroit. The inscription says his greatest contribution to firearms design "was made in 1878 when he completed the development of the 'box magazine.' Tradition holds that this occurred at Wallaceburg while Lee was visiting his brother John, a local foundry owner."

The Odd Couple

Frederick and Frances Hamerstrom were a couple from the East Coast who came to the Midwest and studied at the University of Wisconsin-Madison under Aldo Leopold. They became wildlife researchers for the state Department of Natural Resources, doing most of their work on the Buena Vista Marsh south of Stevens Point. They're both in the Wisconsin Conservation Hall of Fame.

The Hamerstroms zeroed in on the prairie chicken. Their findings were the reason the Department of Natural Resources came to own and manage thousands of acres of habitat on the Buena Vista for the chickens and other grassland species.

The prairie chicken is a big grouse, found statewide after the northern forest was cut and burned, but scarce now. The best population is on the marsh, and the fact that it exists there at all may be due to the Hamerstroms.

Fran (pronounced Frahn) was a former Boston debutante and fashion model and somewhat of a madcap eccentric, but a good researcher. She could write too and was the author of a dozen books on wildlife subjects. One of the books was *Is She Coming Too?*. The title quoted a man who couldn't imagine a woman coming on a hunting trip. She probably outshot him.

The couple lived in a big, shabby-looking, pre-Civil War-era house west of Plainfield and just south of the marsh, but eventually took to spending their winters in Texas because Fred had been frostbitten while working on the marsh and couldn't tolerate the cold. In Texas, they continued their work at the Welder Wildlife Refuge.

The Hamerstroms, being the people they were, didn't spend a lot of money modernizing their old house, which they shared with their son and daughter and assorted wildlife. One of their pets was a grim-looking great horned owl named Porfirio.

Fred and Fran were teachers as well as researchers, and regularly hosted apprentices they called "gabboons," meaning slave in an African language. But it was not involuntary servitude. The "gabboons" learned, and enjoyed while learning. They came from all over this country and abroad, and some of them went on to prominent careers in wildlife management.

Prairie chickens put on a spectacular mating dance in spring and people would crowd into the Hamerstrom home, spend the night there, and go out into the marsh in early morning to watch the birds perform. Over the years, the number of guests that stayed there was in the thousands.

Fran didn't look like the domestic type, but she was a good cook. She once invited me to her home for lunch and it was excellent. She also wrote *The Wild Food Cook Book*, which contained all sorts of recipes for fish, game, and wild plants. Some of them may have been tongue-in-cheek, like her recipes for jack oak patties, lung soup, and fox snake. Or maybe not, knowing Fran.

She told of cutting a road-killed fox snake into three-inch lengths, flouring them lightly and frying them in butter. "Snake is best picked up by the fingers for eating," she wrote. "It is a delicacy to be savored as hors d'oeuvres, or to be served simply with saltines or potato chips." It's easier to eat than fish, she said, because the ribs stick to the backbone.

The Hamerstroms were animal lovers, but they hunted. It's the species that counts, not the individual animals, they said. Fran once said, "Anti-hunters would much rather buy their meat."

Though they focused on the prairie chicken, the couple did research on other birds and mammals, too. It didn't end with their deaths. A kestrel (sparrow hawk) study on the marsh—begun by Fran—is still going on, decades later. The Hamerstroms were sometimes criticized for doing the same research over and over. But Fran said long-term studies are important because there's always something new to learn.

After Fred died in 1990 at the age of 80, Fran kept on with her work. Grief does no one any good, she said. Even in her 80s, she went to Africa and South America to work with pygmies and Indians. She died in 1998 at the age of 91.

DuBay

John Baptiste DuBay was a famous early Wisconsin settler who, among other things, had a trading post north of Stevens Point that's now covered by a big impoundment on the Wisconsin River. The impoundment, appropriately, is named Lake DuBay.

I once saw a document of some sort DuBay had signed. His signature was a big "X". Literate or not, he was said to be the wealthiest person in the area at one time, though when he died in 1887, he was described as a poor man.

DuBay had his rocky moments. He was once tried for murder at Fort Winnebago, near today's city of Portage. The attorney who defended him at the trial got him off on a technicality. That lawyer was Moses Strong, a political finagler who once helped bribe the state Legislature in a matter involving a land grant. Strong spent most of his career in Mineral Point but had land holdings in Stevens Point, and Strongs Avenue is named for him.

DuBay was a respected man in spite of the murder charge, and his obituary said, "beneath that dark, weather-tanned flesh beat a heart that was tender and kind." He came by that dark skin naturally. Though his father was of French extraction, his mother was an Indian.

People

In 1946, Merton E. Krug wrote a book called *DuBay, Son-in-law of Oshkosh*, and in it he called DuBay "a legendary figure of the old pinery lumbering region before Paul Bunyan's fabled exploits were heard of here." The book's title referred to DuBay's reputed marriage to Princess Madeline, daughter of Oshkosh, chief of the Menominee tribe.

Some have questioned whether DuBay and Madeline were really married. The issue came up in a talk given at the University of Wisconsin-Stevens Point by Philleo Nash of Wisconsin Rapids. Nash, a one-time lieutenant governor, commissioner of the U.S. Bureau of Indian Affairs, and an archeologist excavated the DuBay trading post site before it was flooded.

Someone asked Nash if DuBay and Madeline actually were husband and wife. After a pause, he replied, "They said they were married. It was the frontier."

DuBay's grave, topped by an impressive monument, stands along County Highway DB, south of Knowlton and not too far from Lake DuBay.

The lake is a big one, more than 10 square miles. It was something of an eyesore when it was created in 1942 because the trees on the lake bed hadn't been cut. But eventually Consolidated Water Power Co., the owner of the dam, arranged to have a boat with an underwater saw clear the flooded forest.

Once, camping on its shores, I was almost driven away by the smell because of a fish kill caused by low dissolved oxygen. But like other Wisconsin waters, Lake DuBay benefited from the federal Clean Water Act of 1972 and is a lot healthier today. It has a good fish population and is a fitting memorial to John Baptiste DuBay.

Mary Had It Right

A premier program at the University of Wisconsin-Stevens Point is natural resources. Mary D. Bradford didn't start it, but she might be called its spiritual ancestor.

The university was created in 1894 as the Stevens Point Normal School, and Bradford was one of its original faculty members. A distinguished educator, she is believed to have been the first woman superintendent of a major city school district (Kenosha) in the United States. A high school in Kenosha is named for her.

The Stevens Point Normal School didn't have a natural resources program, but Bradford had the same instincts that impelled Fred Schmeeckle to found what became UW-Stevens Point's College of Natural Resources.

Something happened about the time Bradford came to Stevens Point that revealed her deep interest in the environment. It involved what she called a "bit of the forest primeval" which in 1894 stood on the banks of the Wisconsin River north of Stevens Point. Logging and fire had already made deep inroads into the state's forests, but for some reason this woodland was still intact.

In her memoirs she wrote, "This choice natural object brought to my ear for the first time the sound of the wind in the tree tops of the forest, of which poets had told me; and to my feet the feel of soft beds of pine needles. But there was money value in those mighty trees—the growth of centuries."

But then, she wrote, "The rumor reached us that they were to be cut down and sacrificed. Greed would push them into the hungry maw of the screaming sawmill. The weak but earnest protest of some of us faculty members who loved the pines was unheeded. Those wonderful trees are only a memory now – alas! but had those owners been generous and saved them, what a monument would be standing now to commemorate their deed! Or had the citizens had the vision of what such a natural park would add to the attractiveness of their city, and had moved vigorously to keep it intact, that irretrievable loss might have been averted."

But the instincts of the time were to log the Wisconsin forests and when the trees had been cut, move on to another forest.

Bradford was right. Had the pines been saved they'd be a local and state treasure, something to boast about. She hadn't been born in the wilderness. She grew up in Kenosha, in the southeastern corner of Wisconsin, far from the state's great northern forest. Maybe her unfamiliarity with giant pines is what made her appreciate them more than someone who had lived among them all his or her life.

Fred Schmeeckle, who came along in the 1920s, didn't grow up in the deep woods either. He was from Nebraska and arrived in Stevens Point as an agriculture teacher. Here, he came to the conclusion that Wisconsin children needed to know about conservation, and he was a leader in a push to require that it be taught in the state's public schools.

He went a step further and started a program in what was then the Stevens Point State Teachers College to train teachers to teach conservation. The program grew and some of its graduates became leaders in environmental organizations such as the Wisconsin Conservation Department, later to become the Department of Natural Resources.

A large natural area on the UW-Stevens Point campus is named for Schmeeckle.

The Conservation Education Program became the College of Natural Resources and broadened under the leadership of Dan Trainer. Trainer grew up in Princeton, in south-central Wisconsin. Though not in the heart of the forest, it lay in a region of lakes, marshes, and abundant wildlife. Moreover, his father was a warden-supervisor with the Conservation Department.

The College of Natural Resources' graduates are spread around the country and the globe, so the influence of Schmeeckle and Trainer is still felt. And don't forget Mary D. Bradford.

A Link With the Past

Though born and raised in Wisconsin, Minnie Whitewing didn't really speak English. Minnie was a member of the Ho-Chunk tribe, also known as Winnebagos, and she mainly spoke her native tongue. She died in Stevens Point March 16, 1957.

She had been living with a son and daughter near Dancy and was said to be somewhere between 102 and 110 years old, an age that couldn't be confirmed by birth records because they weren't keeping them in those days.

She was able to recall a skirmish near Endeavor between Sioux Indians and her people which historians say occurred in 1851, so an age of 110 was plausible. A physician who treated her in her final illness didn't doubt that she was past 100.

Minnie was born near Tomah and picked up some English while playing with the children of white settlers, but she was never fluent in the language.

Her long life spanned the time from the hunter-gatherers to the jet age. She was buried in an Indian cemetery at Babcock and left many descendants.

We sometimes trace American history only back to 1492, when Columbus landed, or 1620, when the Pilgrims came ashore at

Plymouth Rock. But people were in North America thousands of years before Columbus was born, and Indians were in Wisconsin when the Ice Age was ending some 10,000 years ago.

Jean Nicolet was the first European to make contact with the Ho Chunks. That was in 1634, at a time when they were numerous. Diseases brought by Europeans decimated the Ho-Chunks and other tribes. Ho-Chunk numbers were also said to have been reduced by a storm on Lake Michigan or Lake Winnebago, and by battles with neighboring Indians.

The Ho-Chunks' numbers grew again as they intermarried with other tribes and the French. Today, they have a reservation in Nebraska and a scattered population in Wisconsin.

They kept no written records, so our knowledge of the tribe's early history comes from word of mouth and archeological finds. They may have been the ancestors of the mound builders who left their mark on the land. Many of those mounds have been destroyed, but the remaining ones are protected by law in Wisconsin.

The Indians who inhabited Wisconsin at the time of white settlement didn't have a civilization as elaborate as those of the Mayas, Aztecs, and Incas of Latin America, but they had adapted to their environment. Like us, they didn't always get along with their neighbors, sometimes warring with other tribes, just as we war with other countries.

One notable Wisconsin Ho-Chunk was Cpl. Mitchell Red Cloud Jr., who earned the Medal of Honor (the nation's highest honor for bravery) in the Korean War. He died in the war and a historical marker now honors him on Highway 54 near Black River Falls.

You may have noticed that I use the word "Indian" throughout my essays, though "Native American" may be more politically correct. Here's why:

Ada Deer used to live in Stevens Point and occasionally came into the office where I worked. She was a member of the Menominee Tribe and later headed the U.S. Bureau of Indian Affairs.

One day I asked her whether she was an Indian or a Native American. "I'm an Indian," she said. If that was good enough for Ada Deer, it was good enough for me.

Hornberg

Even though they arrest people, wardens are respected. It's recognized, even by violators of fish and game laws, that they're out there protecting the public's resources.

Sometimes a warden becomes a near-legend, as in the case of Frank Hornberg.

Nowadays, the Wisconsin Department of Natural Resources hires college graduates as wardens. Years ago, the hiring rules were looser, as in Hornberg's case. He prepped for the job by being a locomotive engineer. He had had a touch of tuberculosis and was told he needed to get a lot of fresh air, then considered the best treatment for the disease. So in 1920, he became a warden and was stationed in Portage County.

He was the first warden specifically assigned to the county, and to help him do his job the Portage County Fish and Game Protective Association bought him a Model T Ford, which he equipped with a sleeping bag, cooking utensils, boots, and rain gear. In it, he patrolled the county. He retired about 30 years later when he was almost 70, pretty old to be lying in a snowbank waiting for poachers.

He was big and impressive, with a booming voice. Virgil (Pete) Peters once wrote, "When decked out in his forest green uniform,

Smokey bear hat, shined leather puttees, and shoes, one stood at attention. There are still a few old-timers around whom Hornberg picked up for various violations who tremble and shake at the mere mention of his name."

In Hornberg's day, wardens were the Conservation Department (predecessor of the Department of Natural Resources) in most of the state. That was before the department made heavy use of fish and wildlife biologists and foresters.

It was the warden who decided where the hatchery fish were planted, and Hornberg was a pioneer in stocking trout in inland lakes. He said he had closely studied Sunset Lake in Portage County, determining whether it was suitable for trout in terms of such things as depth and water quality. He decided it could support trout, so he planted them there. It became a popular trout fishery and still is.

Others told a different story. They said Hornberg was out in the country one spring day with a load of hatchery fish for planting in trout streams. The day was warm, the dissolved oxygen in the water was getting low and it appeared that the trout were dying. Rather than let that happen, he dumped them in the nearest body of water, which happened to be Sunset Lake.

You can believe either story, but the fact remains that it was a success and was copied in other Wisconsin lakes.

Hornberg left another heritage—a trout fly he devised and which is called, naturally, the Hornberg. It's fished as both a dry fly and a streamer and is still popular. And a Trout Unlimited Chapter in Central Wisconsin is named in his honor.

Dealing with law violators can get to you, and Hornberg became somewhat cynical toward the end of his career. "There are no more sportsmen," I once heard him mutter (he muttered loudly). He moved to California after retiring, and I sent him a letter asking him to write a few details about his career. He had mellowed, and his response was philosophical. He'd obviously forgiven the game law violators who'd given him so much grief over the years.

Frank Hornberg died in 1966 in Santa Rosa, California, at the age of 84.

Les Was More

Diplomatic Hall of Fame? Les Woerpel would never have made it. Too outspoken.

But he made it into the Wisconsin Conservation Hall of Fame, and with good reason. With his sidekick, Richard Hemp of Mosinee (another Hall of Famer), he founded the Wisconsin Federation of Conservation Clubs, which became today's Wisconsin Wildlife Federation.

And he fought a long, hard battle to keep the Wisconsin Valley Improvement Co. (WVIC) from building a dam on the Little Eau Pleine River. Instead of a big, shallow, fluctuating reservoir, the valley became the Mead Wildlife Area, a heavily used, publicly owned hunting ground and wildlife viewing area.

Would it have happened without Woerpel's delaying tactics? There's a good chance it wouldn't have.

He was admitted to the Hall of Fame in 1990. After his death in 1998, his son, Loren, wrote a letter in which he told of going with his father to meetings concerning the dam and reservoir. "He would work the night shift at AT&T so sometimes he needed a driver," he explained.

Loren was a high school student then. "My remembering," he

said, "was that he really always thought he would win that one (the battle to stop the dam on the Little Eau Pleine)." He said he was amazed that his father, this "telephone guy," stood up as an equal to the big attorneys in front of a hearing judge for the Public Service Commission, the agency then in charge of such things.

If Les Woerpel thought he was going to win that big one, it was a minority opinion. His opposition, the majority, thought otherwise, and they were right, to a point. The Public Service Commission approved the dam, but it didn't get built. Changing economics, and very possibly the delays orchestrated by Woerpel, caused the WVIC to drop the project. Consolidated Water Power & Paper Co., the owner of the 20,000 acres that would have been flooded, gave the land to the state. Now it's the Mead Wildlife Area.

Woerpel did other things for wildlife and the environment, like working to prevent the extirpation of Wisconsin's prairie chickens. And for years he edited "News and Views," a widely read conservation newsletter that didn't hesitate to tackle controversial issues.

Whitetail Doe

MAMMALS

Deer Revival

You can't write about the Wisconsin outdoors and ignore deer. Hunting them is all some people think about, even in the off-season. More than that, deer affect the whole environment, for better and sometimes for worse. Wolves and bears prey on them. Farmers, foresters, and highway travelers may curse them. And hunters, of course, love them.

At one time, Wisconsin's deer population was so low the hunting season was closed, or held only in alternate years, and then only in part of the state. In years when deer hunting was legal, it was restricted to bucks. Does were sacred.

In pre-settlement days, the deer population was kept under control by predators, harsh winters, Indians, and habitat conditions. The old-growth forest in much of the state was not good for deer.

With few hunting regulations and almost no enforcement, settlers increased the assault on deer. They were attracted with salt licks, hunted with dogs, and shot year-round.

Venison was a major part of many people's diets in the 19th century and well into the 20th. A man living alone in the Minocqua area in the 1940s said he could get through the winter all right if he'd saved up $40 in the summer doing odd jobs. He heated his house

Mammals

with wood, which he got free, ate native fruits and berries, fished, and his meat came from the deer he poached. Wardens tended to look the other way if people needed venison to survive and weren't selling it.

Ernest Swift, later director of the Wisconsin Conservation Department (forerunner of the Department of Natural Resources), wrote a history of the state's deer in 1946 and said management of the animal had become "a subject of seemingly endless controversy." Endless, all right. Deer management still is controversial, along with an enormous increase in the deer kill.

In the 1917 season, 18,000 deer were killed in Wisconsin and Conservation Commissioner E.W. Barber asked, "Does any sane man contend that these animals can stand that sort of killing?" In 2000, the state's deer kill was about 600,000.

What had happened was a population explosion, first in the Northern Wisconsin cutover, where the young, rejuvenating forest was an ideal habitat. Deer became so numerous that, when they yarded up in cedar swamps in winter, they largely ruined the vegetation and often starved.

People used to take loads of hay up north to feed them, but they seldom got it back to where the deer were. Besides that, deer were used to eating browse and had trouble digesting hay. And if some deer were saved, this only increased the population problem.

Many hunters still refused to admit deer had become so numerous that they created a problem, and they were abetted by northern tourist interests. People on vacation liked to drive the back roads in the evening, looking for deer. "Save the Doe" clubs were formed to block the repeal of the bucks-only rule. The sentiment was echoed farther south. At a Portage County fish and wildlife rules hearing in 1970, a man argued against the party permit, which allowed does to be shot. "You can't kill the cow and still have it," he argued.

After the iron grip of the one-buck law was broken, deer numbers in the north were gradually brought under control. But the population exploded farther south, where the mixture of farms and forests provided ideal habitat.

A new player in the game is the gray wolf, a hungry predator. It was eradicated from the state by about 1960 but returned, and some hunters claim the wolf is responsible for a serious reduction in the northern deer herd. Others question that, saying other things are to blame and the wolf is a convenient excuse.

There's general agreement that wolf numbers need to be controlled, but many consider the big predator an asset and don't want to eliminate too many of them.

It comes down to a matter of balance. Deer belong here, but their numbers need to be kept at a reasonable level.

Jackass Rabbit

Early settlers called it the jackass rabbit because its long ears reminded them of a donkey. Later it just became the jackrabbit, an animal that's really a hare, not a rabbit. What's the difference? I'll explain later.

Regardless, this once abundant animal has apparently disappeared from the state. In his book, *The Wild Mammals of Wisconsin*, published in 2008, Charles Long wrote, "The white-tailed jackrabbit seems to have vanished from Wisconsin and the reasons are unknown."

It was once found throughout the state and was especially common in a belt across the middle of Wisconsin.

By 1990, jackrabbits were scarce, at best. Joe Haug, a wildlife biologist with the Department of Natural Resources, said, "We don't even have a report of a track."

The jackrabbit is a native American animal, but not necessarily a native Wisconsin animal. Possibly it existed in the western part of the state at the time of settlement, or maybe it was imported from the west. Haug said there was a jackrabbit transfer from South Dakota to the Abbotsford area as recently as the early 1970s but it didn't take well, probably because the habitat wasn't right and the animal was vulnerable to hunting.

Wisconsin had a jackrabbit hunting season until 2007, closing it then, possibly after the animal had disappeared from the state. Jacks weigh up to 14 pounds—three times the size of a cottontail rabbit. They're good game animals and very edible. They still thrive in western states and Canada where there's more open land than in Wisconsin.

Now, about rabbits and hares. Both used to be classed as rodents but the taxonomists decided that wasn't right. Now they're in the *lagomorph* family.

The cottontail rabbit, probably abundant in your garden, is truly a rabbit. The snowshoe rabbit and the jackrabbit are hares.

Hares have longer legs and bigger ears than rabbits. They scrape out depressions in the earth instead of building nests, and their young are born fully furred with their eyes open. Rabbit offspring are born hairless, with their eyes closed.

Deer Don't Stand Still

You don't think of white-tailed deer as migratory animals, but they may move with the seasons. No, not long distances like the birds that nest in the arctic and winter in the tropics, but miles to more sheltered areas when cold weather sets in.

On a Central Wisconsin marsh, the Buena Vista, a University of Wisconsin-Stevens Point graduate student named Bob Murphy studied deer and how they moved.

He found that in spring, does would move to the marsh, where the vegetation greened up early. He reasoned that it gave them a nutritional lift before their fawns were born. They stayed on the marsh through the summer, but in fall moved to wooded areas to the west where the cover was better than on the open marsh. They traveled as far as 17 miles each way.

He caught deer with rocket nets and box traps and ran down a couple of fawns on foot. He put ear tags on the animals for identification by sight, and radio-collared others. He located them every day, riding around in an antenna-equipped car and sometimes using a plane when they were hard to find during spring and fall movements.

He even used his beagle, a dog that loved to chase deer, to find a buck he'd shot with a dart containing a tranquilizer. The dart had a radio transmitter that was supposed to allow the deer to be located while the tranquilizer was taking effect. But the dart fell off, and that's when Murphy resorted to his backup system, the beagle. He and a friend finally found the groggy deer and tied up the dog, but the beagle got loose and jumped on the deer, which took off and escaped. By then it was dark and Murphy was lost. He concluded that the dart gun was not an effective tool.

Murphy confirmed that bucks have a short life span in Central Wisconsin. Fifteen of the deer he radio-collared were buck fawns, and fourteen of them were shot by bow and gunhunters as yearlings. He called the turnover rate of the bucks "unreal."

Despite the heavy kill, deer hold their own through a high reproductive rate. Murphy radio-collared only one adult buck, and from him learned what veteran hunters have always known: An old buck is a smart buck.

He pinpointed its location from radio signals and watched as two hunters walked right by it in a small patch of corn. The buck never moved and the hunters never saw it. Later, several drives through the area failed to move the deer.

The Water Walker

I was fishing for trout on the Tomorrow River when a mouse ran across the stream in front of me. It didn't swim across, it ran.

I wondered if my brain was playing tricks, but then it happened again. I first believed I had witnessed a miracle, but being a little skeptical, I decided to research the issue. When I got home, I consulted Hartley H.T. Jackson's book, *Mammals of Wisconsin*.

I found nothing about mice walking on water, but I kept on reading and came to the shrews, mouse-like animals of which we have several species in Wisconsin. One is the water shrew, and there I found my answer. Jackson said the water shrew can "actually run on the surface of the water with the greatest ease." He wrote that he had seen one run more than five feet on a pond near Rhinelander. I think the ones I saw ran even farther.

I wrote about my water shrew experience and was exposed to considerable ridicule from non-believers. But I also heard from two fishermen who had a similar experience.

Charles Long's, *The Wild Mammals of Wisconsin*, hadn't been published at the time of my water shrew observation, but this book, too, says the animal can run on water. Long wrote that the water's surface tension keeps it up, aided by the animal's light weight, large feet, and bubbles in its fur.

The water shrew definitely is small, a half-ounce or so. The shrew family includes some of the world's smallest mammals.

In Wisconsin, water shrews are found in the southern half and are uncommon even there. The species may be in peril in this state, Long wrote.

Despite their size, water shrews are fierce predators on insects, snails, and small fish. They have to be. Their metabolism is so high they need to eat constantly. They're also preyed upon. A water shrew running across a stream makes a nice between-meals snack for a big trout.

By the way, I once saw another animal run on water. Some years ago, I tagged along on a University of Wisconsin-Stevens Point field trip to Costa Rica. There, I saw a small reptile race across a stream. This creature is known irreverently as the Jesus Christ lizard.

Bounty Hunters

It was once routine to pay a bounty on just about any creature that preyed on game we liked to hunt or on fish we liked to catch. Alaska once had a bounty on the bald eagle because *Our National Symbol* ate salmon.

Wisconsin over the years has had bounties on many creatures, including wolves. The wolf bounty was lifted in the late 1950s, shortly before the animal disappeared from the state, only to reappear in the 1970s.

Although it's generally conceded that Wisconsin now has as many wolves as it needs and then some, don't count on the state paying hunters to kill them. They can be hunted and trapped now that wolves in the upper Midwest are off the endangered list, but it won't be an all-out extermination program. Some people think the wolf is doing us a service by reducing deer numbers and dispersing the animals.

Nor are we apt to see a return to fox bounties, though they hung on longer than the wolf bounty in some parts of the state, including Portage County, where the fox bounty wasn't lifted until 1974. The reason for the bounty was that foxes were suspected of killing things like ruffed grouse and rabbits. More than a suspicion, a fact. But they also eat things that can be pests.

And it can be argued that their impact on game animals is less than natural cycles and habitat loss due to things like urban sprawl. So far, no one has proposed a bounty on city people who move to the country.

Bobcats were bountied in Wisconsin until 1963. Now they get a lot of protection, with a limited hunting and trapping season in just the northern part of the state. Years ago there was even a bounty on the Canada lynx, a rare animal in Wisconsin then and now. A story in the *Stevens Point Journal* in 1916 told of Ed Sherman of the town of Pine Grove shooting one and collecting two $3 bounties, one from Portage County and one from the state. The news story was emphatic that it was a lynx, not a bobcat. Today, the lynx is protected in Wisconsin.

One reason why bounties became unpopular was the belief that fraud was often involved. To prevent this, the ears of bountied animals were clipped so they could be identified in case someone tried to bring in the same animal twice. The women who worked in the county clerk's office hated doing the clipping. And it was alleged that some trappers released female foxes so they could produce more bounty material.

At a time when the fox bounty was a controversial issue, I offered a suggestion. When the price of a fox pelt was high, I wrote, the trapper should pay into a county fund for each one he trapped.

When the price was low, I said, the county should subsidize the trapper out of this fund. There'd be no cost to the public, the trappers would be happy, the taxpayers would be happy, everybody would be happy except the foxes. To my great surprise, the suggestion was not taken seriously.

Here's an example of the right hand not knowing what the left hand was doing: In a book, *The Vanishing Present*, Adrian Wydeven and Charles Pils wrote that the Wisconsin Conservation Department was stocking foxes to provide hunting opportunities at the same time fox bounties were being paid.

For what it's worth, the red fox may not be an all-American animal. Red foxes were here when Europeans arrived, but British colonizers, who loved fox hunting, felt a need to boost the population and imported European red foxes. So the foxes we have today may be Anglo-American hybrids. Tally-ho!

In the days when bounties were in place, not everyone liked to kill the varmints. A story in the *Stevens Point Journal* on April 18, 1923, told of trappers who brought seven wolf cubs to the courthouse and were told they had to kill them to collect the bounty. They didn't like that. They wanted to give the animals to a zoo. Possibly those "wolves" were coyotes. In those days, people often didn't distinguish between the species. Coyotes were frequently called brush wolves.

Wolves and other predators are not on the top of everyone's popularity list today, and they were even more disliked generations ago, even by Aldo Leopold. When he was with the U.S. Forest Service in the Southwest, he favored the extermination of wolves and cougars in order to build up the deer population. He wrote, "It's going to take patience and money to catch the last wolf or [mountain] lion in New Mexico, but the last one must be caught before the job can be called fully successful."

He later wrote, "In those days we never heard of passing up a chance to kill a wolf. I thought that because fewer wolves meant more deer, that no wolves would mean hunters' paradise."

His eyes were opened when he saw plants browsed to death by deer on the Kaibab Plateau in Arizona. After predators were exterminated by government hunters, the mule deer population on the plateau had exploded.

Western writer Zane Grey thought he had the solution. He organized a group of mounted men to drive the deer out of the plateau, into the Grand Canyon and up the other side, where there was plenty of food. I once talked to a man whose father was one of those mounted men. "He learned that deer don't drive," he said, at least not the way Grey wanted them driven.

Getting back to foxes, they've become semi-urban animals. Twice they've been spotted in our city yard and who knows how many other times they visited when we weren't watching. A few years ago, a mallard built a nest in our yard. The eggs disappeared and I asked a Department of Natural Resources wildlife biologist what he thought had happened. Very likely it was a fox, he said. A couple years later, another mallard nested in our yard and brought off a hatch. So I guess ducks can survive predators, though there'll always be losses.

Question: Do bounties work? They didn't in Colorado. Between 1915 and 1947 the state paid about $1.8 million on coyote bounties, but in the end, coyotes were as plentiful as ever. Utah had a similar experience.

The Big, Not-So-Bad, Wolf

If no one else wants to say something nice about wolves, Kevin Burns will. He's the forest ecologist at Treehaven, a 1,400 acre environmental station near Tomahawk operated by the University of Wisconsin-Stevens Point.

Sure, wolves kill deer and sometimes livestock and dogs. But they don't attack people, and Burns thinks they're friends of the forest.

When wolves came back to Wisconsin, the population climbed a lot higher than the target of 350 set by the Department of Natural Resources. In fact, more than twice as high. But efforts to put limits on wolf numbers were thwarted because the wolf was on the federal endangered list.

Animal rights groups kept protesting that the animal really was endangered (no one else thought so). As a result, the issue of wolf population control was tied up in the federal courts and the state couldn't do much.

Now it's off the list and hunting and trapping is allowed. The wolf will continue to prey on deer, which is something big carnivores do. Is that bad? Not entirely. A high deer population is damaging to forests, farms and highway travelers. We like to think of them as "our" deer, but I guess they're the wolves' deer, too.

In Wisconsin, the reproduction of some trees became nearly impossible because of heavy deer browsing. I once asked a man who owned a white cedar swamp if the trees were reproducing. No, he said, and he blamed deer.

Where deer are overly abundant, it's easy to recognize a browse line on trees, but we don't notice other plant damage as long as what's left is green.

Wolves can reduce browsing by deer, not merely by killing them but by keeping them moving. This is helping cedars recover in some northern swamps. Wolves serve a similar purpose at Treehaven. Kevin Burns, the forest ecologist, said most foresters believe overbrowsing by deer is a bigger problem than the public realizes.

"Yes, we can still grow healthy trees and forests even when faced with this severe browsing issue," Burns wrote, "but they are, and will become, much simpler (less diverse) forests as a result of selective browsing pressure. Tree species such as northern white cedar, hemlock, sugar maple, etc. (this is a long list), are not growing through the browse line (greater than six feet in height). Some species are already completely absent from landscapes where they thrived in the past (Canada yew and others). This problem is particularly noticeable in areas with the ultra-high deer populations.

"I would not go as far as to say that the presence of wolves 'prevents' overbrowsing, but I do strongly believe they help to reduce selective browsing pressure. Of course wolves do reduce some of the deer population numbers, but I believe they have an even larger impact on deer movement (or lack of movement), which essentially spreads the browsing over a larger area, and may force them to select more of the less desirable browse species—thus reducing pressure on the more favored browse species.

"I do believe that wolves are definitely an asset to Treehaven, as well as all forest environments. They have had a positive impact on our forests in Wisconsin since re-establishment, and possibly a measurable positive impact on our forest at Treehaven. Wolves are, and should remain, a vital component of our forests in Wisconsin.

So, long story short—it's not that I am a wolf lover, I am more of a lover of anything that reduces the browsing problems we see on our forest resources."

Hartley H.T. Jackson, in his book, *Mammals of Wisconsin*, said the state may have had 20,000 to 25,000 wolves at the time of settlement. Wildlife experts now believe 3,000 to 5,000 is a more accurate estimate. That's still a lot more than the people of the state would tolerate now, but people like Kevin Burns believe we have room for a significant number of wolves as well as a significant number of deer.

The November 1955 issue of the *Wisconsin Conservation Bulletin* carried an article entitled "The Case for the Timber Wolf" written by John Keener, then a Conservation Department game manager at Rhinelander and later the state's superintendent of game management.

At that time, Wisconsin's wolves probably numbered fewer than 50, all in the north, and if you killed one you could collect a $20 bounty. Keener argued that the number of deer eaten by wolves was minor compared with those killed by poachers and motor vehicles. The wolf performed a service, he said, by slowing the growth of the deer herd, though he acknowledged that it wasn't making much of a dent in the population at that point.

One way to keep the wolf from vanishing from the state, Keener wrote, would be to eliminate the bounty. And it was eliminated—right about the time Wisconsin's last wolf died. Another idea, which Keener called more drastic, would be to place the wolf on the protected list. "It is hardly conceivable," he wrote, "that the thinking people of Wisconsin will allow the species to disappear from one of its last homes in the United States." Allow it they did, but the wolf reintroduced itself and is flourishing.

Return of the Natives

Not all the animals that were here when the settlers arrived are still with us, but it's possible to bring some of them back.

The wild turkey has already been successfully reintroduced into Wisconsin.

The elk has been brought back, too. Twenty-five of them from Michigan were released near Clam Lake in 1995, but the herd isn't multiplying as fast as hoped.

The whooping crane has returned but it remains to be seen whether it can establish a reproducing population.

The moose shows up now and then in the northwest part of the state but a hefty deer population keeps its numbers from growing. Deer carry brainworm but aren't much affected by it. But they spread it to moose, and in them it's fatal.

Cougars have been showing up in Wisconsin, coming from the Black Hills of South Dakota, as determined by DNA evidence. They haven't established a breeding population, but that may come.

Ray Anderson, a professor of wildlife at the University of Wisconsin-Stevens Point, was active in the return of several species, notably the elk. He also had some long-shot candidates for reintroduction.

One was the woodland caribou, but he said it needed to be determined whether the animal actually was here at the time of settlement.

Another was the bison, but it's a big, wide-ranging animal that needs a lot of room, and there's not as much of that in the state as there once was. Maybe, Anderson said, we'll have to settle for semi-domesticated bison behind wire.

Another possibility mentioned by Anderson was the wolverine. This animal has the reputation of a ferocious demon of the woods, capable of even chasing bears away from a kill site.

Anderson felt its reputation for viciousness was undeserved, but its reintroduction, he felt, needed to be preceded by a public relations and education campaign.

Anderson was probably the person most responsible for bringing elk back to Wisconsin after an absence of more than a century.

He was also renowned for his work with bears, prairie chickens, pine martens, and a string of other wildlife species. He had a passion for bringing back native animals that had been extirpated, with the possible exception of Tyrannosaurus rex.

The elk (wapiti) is similar to, but slightly larger than the Old World red deer. It was once found throughout most of Wisconsin but was extirpated, probably about 1875. Its early presence in the state is reflected in place names like Elkhorn and Elk Mound, and by the antlers found in lake and stream beds.

Around the time of World War I, the animal was reintroduced in the Trout Lake area in Vilas County but its numbers dwindled and it finally disappeared. Illegal shooting was at least part of the problem.

The latest elk reintroduction took place in 1995 after a long struggle to find a suitable place for the animals. The Ashland area looked good at first but owners of orchards were doubtful. Elk have been known to strip the bark off trees.

Finally, elk from Lower Michigan were released near Clam Lake in Northwestern Wisconsin. Michigan, too, had extirpated its elk, and the ones it had were descendants of animals brought from Wyoming in 1918. They've done all right in Michigan and the state has an elk hunting season, which is also the goal in Wisconsin when and if the population is high enough. But it's not there yet.

Elk aren't animals of the deep woods, but Clam Lake, though in forest country, has some open areas. They're the result of an abandoned U.S. Navy project. During the Cold War, the Navy wanted to create a way to communicate with submerged submarines.

This entailed burying cables in a huge X-shaped swath, and to do that, the Navy cleared a big forest area near Clam Lake. The project, known as ELF (extreme low frequency), was dropped but the big opening remained. It looked good for elk, so that's where the reintroduction took place.

The elk population didn't grow as fast as hoped due to predation by wolves and bears, and highway mortality. Tip for motorists: Drive carefully in elk country. They're a lot bigger than deer and can do a real number on your car.

If all the details can be worked out, another herd of elk may be started in the Black River Falls area in Western Wisconsin and it might do better. For what it's worth, some states have had good luck with elk reintroduction. Kentucky is an example. It now has thousands of elk and they're spilling over into other states.

Anderson, who died in 2000, had an association with UWSP that began when he enrolled as a freshman with the goal of majoring in mathematics. He had grown up in the little town of White Lake in Langlade County, and the outdoors was imprinted on him. At the university he came under the influence of Fred Schmeeckle, the founder of what became the College of Natural Resources, and Bernard Wievel, one of the college's original faculty members. He then switched his career path to natural resources.

After graduation, he was a high school teacher for a few years and returned to UWSP as a faculty member in 1958. He officially retired in 1990 but continued part-time and kept on with his wildlife research.

His impact on the College of Natural Resources, as well as on wildlife, has been long-lasting. He was credited with drawing up the plan that led to the creation of the college's wildlife management major, now one of its premier offerings.

He was a convincing speaker on the subject of elk. I heard him give a talk at a service club luncheon. People at such functions tend to drift away during long-winded programs. Ray gave a lengthy talk but no one left.

Mammal Count

It's not likely you could name all of Wisconsin's wild mammal species. In fact, it would be hard to agree on the number.

The number is a little fuzzy for several reasons. One is that we have species and we have sub-species. Also, we have animals like the house mouse and the Norway rat which aren't native, but have become established.

We have mammals like the elk that were extirpated but have been brought back. Bison, too, have been brought back, but they're behind fences and aren't free-roaming.

Charles Long wrote a book, *The Wild Mammals of Wisconsin*, and at the time it was published (2008) there were reports of cougars in Wisconsin but they hadn't been authenticated. Since then there have been confirmed reports, but at this writing there was no proven breeding population.

Some Wisconsin mammals, like the white-tailed deer, the cottontail rabbit, and the gray squirrel, are familiar to everyone. But what about the star-nosed mole, the silver-haired bat, and the arctic shrew? They're part of our native wildlife, too, though you may never have seen them, or didn't recognize them if you did.

Some mammals are found only in limited areas of the state or have been seen rarely, like the eastern spotted skunk. The fisher and the pine marten were extirpated long ago but, like the elk, have been reintroduced.

It's not a static situation. Hartley H.T. Jackson's book, *Mammals of Wisconsin*, was published in 1961 and some things have changed since then. Jackson wrote that the white-tailed jack rabbit was fairly common in suitable habitat in much of Wisconsin, but Long, in his book, said it seems to have disappeared from the state.

Frequent Roadkill

We haven't seen any possums in our yard lately, but I imagine they're around. They didn't used to exist in Central Wisconsin but they moved north, though they're not really equipped to handle our winter weather. Frostbitten possum ears and tails are not uncommon.

The possum, more formally known as the Virginia opossum, is a wide-ranging animal, found coast to coast in the United States, up into Canada and down as far as Costa Rica. It's solitary and nocturnal.

A possum used to show up in our yard at night, stumbling around clumsily and eating stuff that fell from a bird feeder. It's an almost defenseless animal and according to the familiar story it sometimes survives by playing possum—pretending to be dead.

Under the best of circumstances it has a short life span and often winds up as a middle-of-the-road animal, squashed by a car on that yellow stripe that runs down the center of a highway. It compensates by having a high birth rate, and is said to be immune to rattlesnake bites.

Charles A. Long, in *The Wild Mammals of Wisconsin*, wrote that the possum's chief enemies in this state are people, dogs, automobiles, and long, cold winters.

Mammals

Despite its vulnerability, the animal has survived almost unchanged for millions of years. Virginia possums and their relatives are the western hemisphere's only marsupials, a type of mammal otherwise found just in Australia and nearby islands.

Captain John Smith of the Jamestown Colony described it this way in the early 1600s:

"An opassum hath an head like a Swine, and a taile like a Rat, and is of the bignes of a Cat." If you overlook the captain's quaint spelling, that's not a bad description.

In Wisconsin, the possum is an unprotected species, meaning you can trap and hunt it without a license. You can sell its fur, but you won't get much for it. And you can eat it, although around here, not many do. But in *Mammals of Wisconsin*, Hartley H.T. Jackson wrote that in the South, "Roasted with sweet potatoes or yams, it is considered a great delicacy."

Maybe we don't eat it here because we never got used to the idea. It was found in Southern Wisconsin when the first settlers arrived, but it apparently didn't start moving north until the 1920s.

Photo courtesy of UW-Stevens Point Archives
George Becker, author of *Fishes of Wisconsin*, examines fish specimens.

FISH LIFE

Musky Luck

A musky fisherman has to be skillful with his fishing rod and knowledgeable about his prey. And a little dumb luck doesn't hurt.

Jim Rowe, Elmer Sbertole, and I were fishing on a northern lake on a warm and bright spring day when the walleyes weren't biting. Elmer had brought a can of worms, so we lowered our expectations and decided to try for panfish.

I hardly had my bait in the water before the bobber went under. It was just a small bluegill, but then we saw a silver flash. A musky had hit the bluegill, knocking it loose and hooking itself.

From a fisherman's standpoint, the outlook wasn't promising. The hook was small (No. 8), the rod was light, and the monofilament line was six-pound test.

This wasn't a monster musky but it was big enough to snap the monofilament if I'd tried to horse it in. All I could do was keep a tight line while Jim, at the oars, kept the boat away from sunken logs where the fish could entangle the line.

A half hour went by and the fish showed no signs of tiring. It still seemed fresh a half hour later. Still another half hour went by and the musky was weakening. I began to believe we might land it, so

I advised my companions to close the tackle boxes because the fish would thrash around if we got it in the boat.

We weren't after muskies, but we fortunately had a good-sized landing net along. Finally we got the fish close enough for Jim to scoop it up and bring it in. It was more tired than I'd thought and hardly moved on the bottom of the boat. This happened before catch and release became popular, so I kept the fish. The musky was so exhausted it might not have made it anyway if I'd let it go.

It was 40 inches long, nice but not spectacular. Not big enough for a full body mount in my opinion, and besides, I wasn't anxious to hang it over the fireplace. But I had an acquaintance who dabbled in taxidermy and he mounted the head only. I still have it, hanging in the basement, with the No. 8 hook dangling from its mouth. Since it's only the head, I can tell people it was 50 inches long and there's no way to disprove it.

The bluegill the musky hit must have looked like a cripple, an easy meal, so I got to thinking a wounded bluegill plug might make a good lure. I carved one, painted it, and attached treble hooks.

I tried it out on the same lake I'd fished before, and sure enough, a musky followed it to the boat, but turned away without hitting it. It wasn't a really good-looking plug in my estimation, and if muskies could laugh, this one was probably chuckling.

Walleyes

I once attended a talk by Babe Winkelman, a Minnesota professional sport fisherman (yes, there is such a thing) and a speaker on angling topics, and I asked him for his definition of an ideal walleye lake. He said he'd never been asked that question before. But scratching his head, he came up with an answer. He said it should cover thousands of acres, be very deep, with a sand, gravel, and rock bottom and lots of forage fish.

That made sense, especially when it comes to size. A big lake will have a lot of wave action to oxygenate walleye eggs. A flowing stream will accomplish the same thing.

Few, if any, lakes in Wisconsin meet all of Winkelman's standards, but a walleye lake doesn't have to be perfect to do the job. The Wisconsin record walleye is an 18-pounder caught in 1933 on High Lake in Vilas County, 734 acres and 31 feet deep.

Walleye fishing is best in the evening or on overcast days, especially in spring. But walleyes don't always play by the rules. Once, fishing on a Northern Wisconsin lake in the middle of a warm, sunny, mid-summer day, I ran into a school of walleyes hungrily feeding near the surface. But that was a quirk. Those normally are the worst possible conditions for walleye fishing.

Fish Life

Muskies get more publicity, but walleyes are probably a more popular sport fish. They don't get nearly as big as muskies and don't fight like a trout or a bass, but they're hard to beat at the dinner table.

In Wisconsin, the walleye has been extensively stocked statewide. Walleye spawning runs in the Fox-Wolf River system are famous. The fish come out of Lake Winnebago and spawn in marshes along the rivers. Similar but less publicized runs occur on other waters.

In lakes, walleyes spawn in shallow water in early spring. That is where Chippewa tribesmen spear them under provisions of 19th century treaties that once resulted in near-violence on Northern Wisconsin waters.

The typical walleye has a 7-year lifespan, but an 18-year-old fish weighing 10.25 pounds was caught in the Wisconsin River near Rhinelander in 1934.

Walleyes are predators and small fish make up most of their diet. That's why walleye fishermen rely heavily on minnows for bait. But they'll bite on lots of other kinds of live bait, and on artificials too. Or on a jig and a minnow, a combination of an artificial and live bait. Don't bother fishing for them with dry flies, however. Now I'll probably hear from someone who caught one on a Royal Coachman.

The walleye has a close relative in some Wisconsin waters, the sauger. It's smaller than the walleye but similar. A still smaller relative is the yellow perch, a favorite at fish fries.

The Fish Book

"It's my legacy," George Becker said. He meant *Fishes of Wisconsin*, a book he had written. A big legacy it is, not just in size – 1,000 pages plus – but in its scientific value.

Becker retired in 1979 as a biology professor at the University of Wisconsin-Stevens Point and continued to work on his book, published in 1983 by the University of Wisconsin Press.

The actual writing was just part of it. What preceded it was years of research. He and his sons, Kenneth, Dale, and David, spent summers seining lakes and streams to learn what fish they held. "It started out as a family effort," he said, "because there was no money for this sort of thing." He dedicated the book to "four wonderful and long-suffering people," his boys and his wife Sylvia.

His biology students helped too, spending weekends collecting fish around the state and doing laboratory work under his supervision.

The book describes 157 existing and extirpated Wisconsin fish species. It includes details such as the number of scale rows around the body just in front of the dorsal fin of the large-scale stoneroller. Pretty dull stuff, unless you're a fisheries biologist.

But Becker also included a lot of anecdotal material and some fishing tips, like the fact that the largemouth bass can distinguish colors and prefers red. He put this in the book despite some opposition from the publisher, because he said he wanted it to be of interest to the fisherman and naturalist as well as to the fishery biologist.

Okay, but what did the real experts, as opposed to the reel experts, think of *Fishes of Wisconsin*?

A few comments:

"One of the best three or four books of its kind ever written." – *Rudolph J. Miller, American Zoologist*

"Clearly the best available regional or state fish book." – *Library Journal*

"This magnificent, encyclopedic reference to 157 fish species—which are found not only in Wisconsin but also in much of the Great Lakes region and Mississippi River watershed—has been a model for all other such works. In addition to comprehensive species accounts, Becker discusses water resources and fisheries management from both historical and practical policy perspectives. The ultimate reference guide for researchers, fish managers, students, and, of course, fishermen." – *Wisconsin Trails* magazine

Fishes of Wisconsin didn't go flying off the shelves at book stores. The price, $75, was intimidating, and so was the book's size. Its bulk discouraged people from curling up in bed with it. But it remains a standard reference book for those who work with fish and is likely to remain so long after most best-sellers are forgotten.

Becker died in 2002 at the age of 85. His life was not without controversy. He tangled with the Wisconsin Department of Natural Resources over such things as chemical treatment to eradicate rough fish (a term he hated).

He had an especially big battle with the DNR over the treatment of the Tomorrow-Waupaca River in the early 1970s. The aim was to eradicate carp and improve the stream for trout, but Becker argued that it would have unintended side effects, such as the eradication of other aquatic species, some of them rare.

He lost the battle. The Tomorrow-Waupaca chemical treatment took place, but since then, the DNR has been more cautious when using this technique.

Becker fought with the DNR on other issues but didn't entirely blame the agency. Sometimes it did what it did, he said, because of pressure from the public.

Becker was deeply involved in pollution control and came up with a plan, which came to be known as Becker's Pipe Dream, to clean up the Wisconsin River. It called for piping municipal and industrial wastes to a series of sophisticated treatment plants and then pumping the purified water back to its source. It didn't happen that way but the Wisconsin River is much cleaner now.

He warned that groundwater pumping for irrigation in Central Wisconsin could reduce stream flows and harm fish. Sure enough, it happened.

So-called "rough fish" are generally harmless, he said, and are a good food source. Even carp have their merits, he contended. We might as well use them for sport and food, said Becker, because they're not going away.

He approved of catch and release fishing and frowned on fishing tournaments because he believed angling should be "a quiet, enjoyable, and private outdoor recreation."

In spite of being outspoken, or maybe because of it, George Becker is in the Wisconsin Conservation Hall of Fame.

The Poetic Justice

Decisions handed down by the judiciary can be pretty dull stuff unless you're one of the litigants. But William Bablitch, a justice of the Wisconsin Supreme Court, waxed almost lyrical in 1995 in the case of the *County of Adams v. Romeo*.

The case involved fishing, and Bablitch wrote what nearly amounted to an ode to angling. Here's what he said:

"Fishing is many things, the least of which to many who indulge is the catching of fish.

"It is, in the winter doldrums, the casual browsing through the fishing catalogs, the fisherperson's equivalent of the gardener's seed catalogs, contemplating the coming renewal;

"It is the snap of a twig across the lake on a dew filled morning signaling the approach of a deer taking the first sip of the dawn;

"It is the desolate cry of the loon signaling its mate in a most haunting communion indecipherable to mere humans;

"It is the screech of the owl ten feet above the river bend warning the invader of its displeasure as we approach at dusk to witness the fleetingly hypnotic hatch of the mayfly, ironically renewing itself at the moment of its demise;

"It is the swish swish swish of the giant wings of the heron as it rises reluctantly from its shallow water preserve, glaringly reminding us that this is its home, not ours.

"It is all this, and more, that brings us back again and again. This is fishing; the catching of a fish is merely ancillary.

"An artificially constructed pond within yards of a natural waterway, 100 feet long, 30 feet wide, and three feet deep into which is put a corn- or pellet-baited hook with sufficient strength of line to water ski a polar bear is not fishing."

Have I mentioned that Bill Bablitch was a fisherman?

Rough Fish

When you catch a big fish, you're apt to brag about it, but maybe not if it's a dogfish. Generally, catching one is no cause for celebration. Dogfish have no class, yet they're a native species that does us some good by thinning out stunted panfish, allowing the survivors to grow faster and larger. But they're not gourmet items.

Dogfish can get pretty big, maybe close to 15 pounds. They're primitive and ancient, said to be contemporaries of the dinosaurs. They're dogged fighters (pardon the pun) and have the unique ability to come up for a gulp of air when the dissolved oxygen in the water is low. The male of the species is a good family man. He protects the dogfish eggs and fry.

While fishing for something else on the Wisconsin River, Gil Oelke and I once caught a dogfish, also known as the bowfin. We released it so it could continue its important work of assassinating undersized panfish. Besides, we didn't want to eat it because dogfish are reputed to taste awful.

Years ago, Vern Hacker of the Department of Natural Resources assembled a collection of recipes in a booklet called *A Fine Kettle of Fish*, in which he praised the flavor of most so-called rough fish. But the best he could say about the dogfish was that it's "generally not considered a good food fish." If you insist on eating it, he suggested freezing it for a month to harden its soft flesh, and then smoking it.

Others say the smell will drive you out of the room when you're cooking it.

The dogfish's looks are against it, with Hacker referring to its "reptilian" head. But the burbot, also known as the lawyer or ling, is likewise unattractive and it's considered good eating. It's the only freshwater member of the cod family, and like the dogfish, is present in the Wisconsin River system.

Speaking of burbots, how do you catch them? Usually by accident, I guess. Hacker said they're normally caught by ice-fishermen using minnows while fishing for walleyes.

With a burbot, said Hacker, the first thing you should do is skin it, though he doesn't explain why. Then fillet it. Burbot, he wrote, is "excellent" pan-fried and "superb" when boiled. Burbot livers, according to Hacker, are reputed to taste better than calves' livers.

A Fine Kettle of Fish, Hacker's booklet, was published in 1982 and is out of print. That's too bad because it contains a lot of useful recipes and is fun to read even if you aren't a cook.

In general, Hacker said rough fish are "delicious, nutritious, and economical" and available in millions of pounds. The recipes in the booklet, Hacker wrote, were contributed by "enthusiastic and unselfish cooks" who wished to pass them on to others. Hacker himself contributed a recipe for fish chowder, calling for four pounds of boned fish along with potatoes, a big onion, salt and pepper, butter, tomatoes, tomato soup, half-and-half coffee creamer, and crackers.

Among the fish for which he provided recipes were carp, buffalo, freshwater drum (sheepshead), burbot, suckers, redhorse, quillback, and gar. He offered suggestions on how to catch them and how to prepare them for cooking.

Example: Some rough fish (and northern pike, too) have many small "Y" bones. "After filleting and skinning," Hacker wrote, "the fillet should be scored by cutting into the fillet and through the 'Y' bones every 1/4 to 1/8 inch ... in the front 2/3 of the fish. Cooking oils are then able to penetrate to the bones to soften them so they cannot be detected."

A nice thing about burbots, he wrote, is that they have no "Y" bones.

Hacker's booklet also has recipes for snapping turtle and crayfish, and it has designs for a crayfish trap and a smoker made from an old refrigerator.

To Set a Record, Lower Your Sights

F orget about catching the state record musky or brook trout. Too difficult. Set a lower goal, like the biggest golden shiner.

And instead of showering praises only on glamor fish, show a little respect for species like the sucker.

The Wisconsin record golden shiner was caught four times in 2011, the last time by Ryan Rejret of Watertown. He caught the fish on Lake Emily in Dodge County. The previous record was set hours earlier on the same lake by Rejret's fiancée, Kristi Fredrich. I didn't hear the length of Rejret's wall-hanger, but it apparently was a bit over 10 inches. The weight was a whopping 7.38 ounces.

The golden shiner is a minnow. It is common to abundant and its average length is about four inches, showing that Rejret's fish really was a giant in its class.

The golden shiner has value. It's part of the food chain for other fish, including muskies, and is also eaten by birds such as herons. It's an excellent bait minnow and eats mosquito larvae in stagnant water. You have to love a fish like that.

Still, I haven't heard of anyone starting a Golden Shiners Unlimited organization. Nor Mud Minnows Forever.

And suckers? Way down on the status list in the eyes of most people. But they shouldn't be. Other fish and herons eat them, and people do, too. They think they're good eating.

Many musky fishermen like them in spite of their looks because they're good bait. People have probably caught more muskies on suckers than on bucktails.

The Fly Tackle Capital

Fly fishing has undergone a revival after a big slump. If it had hung on a while longer before nose-diving, the Wisconsin fly tying industry might have survived.

Foreign imports were one of the things that killed the industry. Fly tying is handwork, not mass production, so low-paid, outsourced labor made it difficult for American companies to compete.

Spinning tackle was another factor. In the post-World War II years, many fishermen turned to spinning rods, reels, and lures, even for trout fishing.

This was heresy for the most dedicated trout fishermen, who saw it as only a small step above the use of garden hackle (earthworms). But enough anglers converted to spinning tackle to help destroy Stevens Point's reputation as the fly tackle capital of America.

At the peak, five companies were tying fishing ties in Stevens Point and 500 fly tyers were at work in the city. All, or nearly all, were women. The manufacturers said their fingers were more nimble than men's. And to be truthful, in those days, women generally worked for less. The tyers made an estimated 10 million flies a year.

Carrie Frost started it in 1896. Unusual for the times, she was an outdoorswoman who hunted and fished. Her father, John Frost, was a trout fisherman who got his flies from England. The story goes that one year his shipment was late, so Carrie tied some for him. They worked, and other fishermen asked her for them.

Carrie persuaded the family maid and other women to help, and an industry was born. They used British patterns but then began tying flies that imitated American insects. She called her business C.J. Frost Co., perhaps to disguise the fact that she was a woman in a male-dominated sport.

Her brother George joined the company and later started his own fly tying business, G.W. Frost & Sons.

Then came Oscar Weber, whose Weber Lifelike Fly Company absorbed Carrie Frost's company. Weber built the firm into the biggest of them all. His company bought feathers by the barrel, literally, and made half the flies tied in Stevens Point.

Weber was a merchandiser as well as a manufacturer, and he had a fleet of salesmen who worked hard to popularize fly fishing. One of them, Bill Cook, claimed to have taught more people to fly cast than any other person alive.

You don't need an advanced degree to fly cast, but it's trickier than spin casting, and that's another reason why the fly tying business dwindled.

When the demand for flies declined, the Weber Company began making plastic products—coolers and the like—but it seemed that everyone was making them, so the company succumbed in 1985.

All the other fly tackle companies are gone too, except the Worth Co., founded by Joseph Worth. His company made a successful transition to fishing tackle components such as split rings.

Some of the flies tied in Stevens Point were designed by local people. One of them, still popular, is the Hornberg, invented by a legendary conservation warden, Frank Hornberg. It's still available in tackle shops and through catalogs.

But Young's Special, named for Oscar Young, a fisherman of note, has been forgotten, except perhaps by a few anglers who tie their own.

In my opinion, the best bass fly ever created was designed by A.J. Koshollek of Stevens Point. Called the Bass-Houn, it had one big fault. It was so big and hairy and offered so much wind resistance that you needed a long, stiff fly rod, a heavy line, and a short leader to cast it, and even then it didn't go far. But it caught fish.

As mentioned above, fly fishing has made a comeback. More fishermen realize it's not really that difficult to master the art. And they believe it's more fun and more sporting than most other types of fishing.

A lot of fishermen now tie their own flies, nimble fingers or not.

Don't Like 'em? Then Eat 'em

They meant well, those people who imported carp from Europe in the 19th century and released them in our waters. It's a valued fish over there. Izaak Walton, an Englishman, called carp the queen of the waters.

But here it became a pest, uprooting aquatic vegetation and damaging the habitat of other fish species and waterfowl.

Carp, fortunately, aren't a problem everywhere. They thrive best in shallow, warm waters and don't do well in fast running streams. But in waters they like, eradicating them is a formidable task.

If you can't lick 'em, cook 'em. That's what they're recommending when it comes to invasive species like the lionfish that's devastating other fish on the reefs along the Florida coast. It looks ugly but tastes good.

People who've tried carp say they don't taste bad either. But the majority won't eat them just because they're carp, or because they're ugly looking. But so are catfish, and people eat plenty of them.

George Becker, author of *Fishes of Wisconsin*, thought carp should be used as food. "When properly prepared, the meat of carp is excellent," he wrote.

Huge numbers of carp used to be seined from Lake Petenwell on the Wisconsin River and shipped to the East Coast for consumption. This ended when contamination made the carp unsafe to eat.

Vern Hacker, in his booklet, *A Fine Kettle of Fish*, said the carp "is considered a delicacy in its native Asia and Europe." He included a number of recipes for carp—baking, broiling, pickling, canning, and more.

Hacker said canned carp tastes like salmon, adding, "Good with crackers and beer as an appetizer." Here's his canned carp recipe, donated by Agnes Trehey of Wauzeka, Wisconsin:

> Fillet carp, chunk, soak in salt water overnight. Wash in fresh water, then pack in pint jars. To each jar add 1-1/2 tsp. canning salt, 1 tbsp. white vinegar, 1 tbsp. tomato sauce, and 1 tbsp. cooking oil. Pressure cook for 90 minutes at 10 pounds pressure (or 65 minutes at 15 pounds pressure).

And here's a recipe for baked stuffed carp, donated by Mrs. Delbert Heschke of Tomahawk, Wisconsin, using a one- to six-pound dressed carp with head, tail, fins, skin, and scales removed:

> Score the fish to break down "Y" bones if you wish. Stuffing: One quart bread crumbs or cubes, 3 tbsp. minced onion, 2 tbsp. ground sage, ¾ tsp. salt, ¾ tsp. pepper, ¾ cup finely chopped celery, and 6 tbsp. hot melted butter. Mix all ingredients well until bread is moistened. Stuff the fish. Place stuffed fish on aluminum foil in a baking dish in oven pre-heated to 500 degrees F. Let brown for 10 minutes, remove, and cover carp with bacon slices. Lower heat to 425 and bake 35 minutes. Add five minutes per pound for carp larger than six pounds.

Fish Potpourri

According to a 1969 survey, there were at least 71 fish species in the lakes and streams of a single Wisconsin county, Portage.

The list included the species familiar to all fishermen, like walleyes, bass, trout, northern pike, bluegills, and many more.

Others were almost unknown and were thought to be inconsequential by most people. They had crazy names like quillback, largescale stoneroller, horneyhead chub, roseyface shiner, banded killifish, and Johnny darter. Are you familiar with any of these?

Also included were several native lamprey species that were causing no particular problem, unlike the sea lamprey that devastated fish in the Great Lakes. Muskies were on the list, but catching one in Portage County was a rare event. It's not so rare anymore thanks to stocking and a much cleaner river.

Sturgeon were not listed, though they'd once been in the Wisconsin River here, but there were unconfirmed reports of sightings. They're definitely there now as a result of an ongoing reintroduction program.

The list of 71 species may have been incomplete, as not all the county had been surveyed thoroughly.

The fish faced threats from siltation, chemicals, and road-building. Effluent from municipalities and industries was causing pollution, but it has been considerably abated since then as a result of steps taken under the Federal Clean Water Act of 1972. A problem lurking in the wings was the impact of irrigation wells on stream flow.

Many of the species on the county list were found only in lakes or small streams, but the Wisconsin River had a good assortment too, as was shown in surveys between 1979 and 1981 by Consolidated Papers and Nekoosa Papers. Their samplings showed 39 species between the DuBay and Petenwell dams, a 70 mile stretch.

A fish that showed up frequently was the walleye, one of which weighed 11.5 pounds. A northern pike weighed 19 pounds.

The mills also interviewed fishermen and reported that 66% said fishing was improving, and 77% said the flavor of the fish was getting better. That made the paper companies happy. They had just spent millions cleaning up their discharges into the river.

Unglamorous, but ...

The sucker family of fish includes many species and they come in many sizes with many names, like quillback and redhorse. Most are of middling weight, but the state record for one variety, the bigmouth buffalo, is better than 73 pounds, heavier than the record musky. It was caught in 2004 in Lake Koshkonong in Jefferson County.

The white sucker is the best-known member of the family, at least around Wisconsin. It's considered a rough fish, but some anglers target it because it's good-eating. Suckers are usually caught on worms and are decent fighters.

George Becker, in his book, *Fishes of Wisconsin*, said the white sucker is probably the state's most widespread fish and isn't overly fussy about water quality. But it isn't a glamor fish and some people avoid eating it because it doesn't have the mystique of a walleye or a brook trout. Years ago, a Michigan company canned them, but though they tasted all right, they couldn't compete with canned salmon.

The flesh of the white sucker, Becker wrote, is "white, sweet, and good tasting, though not as firm as that of most sport species." He called it "a delicacy when smoked."

The white sucker is found anywhere from cold water trout streams to warm water mill ponds. It's a bottom feeder and it used to be accused of preying heavily on musky and walleye eggs. But an examination of the stomachs of several hundred suckers and redhorses found few eggs.

Suckers spawn in spring when the water temperature gets to about 45 degrees, and a big female may lay more than 100,000 eggs. A mark against suckers, from a fisherman's standpoint, is that they compete with game fish for space and food. But they're also prey for game fish.

A popular, though not overly sporting, fishing technique was to use a big sucker as bait and let a musky grab it and slowly swallow it. Only then would the angler set the hook and reel it in. If the musky was undersized, the line would be cut and the fish released in the belief that the hook in its intestines would gradually dissolve and the musky would survive.

But research showed that gut-hooked muskies died. Now quick-strike rigs and circle hooks are required when fishing with large minnows such as suckers. Quick-strike rigs allow an immediate hook-set, and circle hooks are designed to hook the fish in the jaw.

If you're a sucker fisherman, you probably have your own way of preparing and cooking them. If not, Vern Hacker's book, *A Fine Kettle of Fish*, has suggestions for suckers and redhorse. It says they have many "Y" bones and "are best prepared by filleting, skinning, and scoring prior to pan frying, or by freezing the skinned fillets, then running them through a food grinder twice to break down the "Y" bones. The resulting ground fish can be used in patties, hash, or sausage. Both species are also excellent pickled and canned."

He had several sucker recipes. Here's the one for pan-fried suckers:

"Mix 2 parts wheat flour, 1 part pumpernickel rye flour, and 1 part corn meal. Mix well, then shake sucker fillets in the mixture using a paper bag. Lay fillets on a rack for about one-half hour. Flour will absorb moisture. Heat oil or fat. Then shake fish in flour again before dropping into the pan."

Photo by USFWS Mountain Prairie, Greg Kramos, available under the Creative Common License
Greater Prairie-Chickens in the Flint Hills

BIRD LIFE

Egg Salad

The egg collection in the Museum of Natural History at the University of Wisconsin-Stevens Point couldn't be duplicated today. You can get a permit to collect, but only for scientific purposes. And even if you have a permit, what are your chances of finding an egg from the extinct passenger pigeon or the possibly extinct ivory-billed woodpecker?

The eggs at the university were collected in the late 19th and early 20th century by August Schoenebeck. Egg collecting was a popular hobby then, but Schoenebeck was no hobbyist. He was a curator at the Milwaukee Public Museum and he had scientific reasons. He kept careful records on what he collected and where.

His collection got to the university by a circuitous route. He had a friend in this area, Monsignor Julius Chylinski, then pastor of St. Mary of Mt. Carmel Catholic Church in Fancher and later of St. Peter Church in Stevens Point. Schoenebeck was looking for a permanent home for his eggs and, at the priest's suggestion, gave them to the Sisters of St. Joseph in Stevens Point. And the sisters gave them to the university in 1970.

Egg collecting was made illegal because it was pursued so avidly that it threatened the survival of certain species. But later on, egg collections helped save some species.

Comparing eggs in collections with those being laid currently helped prove that the egg shells of fish-eating birds like the bald eagle were becoming thin and breaking, almost ending reproduction. It was determined that the cause was DDT. Its use was tightly controlled and the birds rebounded.

The Schoenebeck collection consists of more than 4,000 eggs from more than 600 species. Some are from foreign countries—Schoenebeck must have traded. But most are of United States origin, including many from Wisconsin.

The collection shows how bird's eggs became adapted to nesting conditions. Killdeer eggs are camouflaged to match the litter in the fields where the birds nest. Cliff-dwelling birds lay eggs with pointed ends so they roll in a tight circle and don't go over the edge. Cavity-nesting birds lay white eggs. Easier to see in the dark.

The eggs come in many sizes, from the tiny ones laid by hummingbirds to the huge ones laid by ostriches. An even larger one was laid by the long extinct elephant bird of Madagascar. It was football-size. The museum doesn't have one, nor does anyone else, although the Smithsonian Institution has fragments.

The elephant bird may have inspired the legend of the roc, although the roc flew and the elephant bird didn't. Too heavy.

The Missing Bird

In 1882, nine Stevens Point hunters took the now defunct Portage Line train to Coloma and, according to a newspaper account, brought back a thousand passenger pigeons.

Not every hunter was that successful. Another newspaper story said a party of 14 hunters went to Coloma after the peak of nesting and shot "not over 200."

In 1914 the last passenger pigeon in the world died in the Cincinnati Zoo, but you can see one (stuffed) in the Natural History Museum in the Albertson Learning Resources Center at the University of Wisconsin-Stevens Point. A passenger pigeon egg is there too.

It was difficult to believe that a species so abundant had been erased from the face of the earth. For decades, people had written about flocks so numerous they darkened the sky. This story was repeated so often it must not have been an exaggeration.

A.W. Schorger of the University of Wisconsin-Madison wrote a detailed book about the birds. They were dreaded in New England in the 1600s because they beat down and ate a lot of domestic grain. But they were also a blessing because they were an easily obtained source of food.

In their heyday, passenger pigeons are said to have numbered between three billion and five billion in the United States and southern Canada. They nested in huge colonies, with the location changing from year to year. In 1871, a nesting stretched from Black River Falls to Wisconsin Dells and north to the Wisconsin Rapids area.

The birds were so numerous their weight broke tree limbs. They ate acorns, beech nuts, berries, insects, and domestic grains. They damaged crops, but their droppings fertilized the soil. People used their feathers to stuff mattresses and pillows.

When they flew out of their nesting areas to feed, flocks were miles long. Often the birds flew so low they could be netted or knocked down with clubs. They were slaughtered by market hunters.

While some people regarded the passenger pigeon as a pest, not everyone approved of the massacre. During the 1882 nesting in Wisconsin, a petition was sent to Governor Jeremiah Rusk, asking him to call out the militia to protect the birds.

Rusk had once activated the National Guard to keep the peace in a Milwaukee labor strike, and it resulted in the guardsmen shooting several strikers. In defense of his actions, Rusk uttered the immortal words, "I seen my duty and I done it." But apparently he had seen no need to protect the passenger pigeons and had done nothing about it. Despite his shortcomings as a grammarian and his questionable judgment in using the militia as strikebreakers, Rusk County in Northwestern Wisconsin is named for him.

The last attempted colonial passenger pigeon nesting in Wisconsin was in 1884 in a swamp north of Wautoma. The birds left because of shooting.

Unrestricted hunting and disruption of nesting are blamed for the pigeons' extinction, but there may have been other reasons—cutting of nut-bearing trees, catastrophic weather, and disease. Also, the birds may have laid no more than one egg per season, and there may have been something about the species that precluded nesting except in huge colonies. When their numbers declined, that may have ended reproduction.

Passenger pigeons looked a lot like mourning doves, and when a Wisconsin dove hunting season was proposed, the passenger pigeon extinction was used as a warning. The season was approved anyway and has had no noticeable effect on the state's dove population.

Of course, mourning doves don't nest in big, vulnerable colonies, and season lengths and bag limits are controlled.

Symbol of Peace?

The controversy has faded, but when a Wisconsin mourning dove hunting season was proposed, it was like lighting the fuse on a stick of dynamite.

The Department of Natural Resources didn't want to touch it, though they said the hunting season had no biological objection and wouldn't endanger the survival of this prolific species. One DNR official told me the agency wouldn't lead the charge because "we tried it years ago and we really got bloodied."

The dove hunting advocates persisted and in 1989, they presented a pro-hunting petition to the state Natural Resources Board, which responded with a unanimous "no," though at that time the majority of American states had dove seasons.

The problem was, many people saw mourning doves as songbirds, not game birds. The Wisconsin Legislature had even designated it as a symbol of peace in an obvious effort to forever quash any attempts to legalize dove hunting.

Some people thought it was unethical to hunt birds that nested in their yards, but others wondered why a dove was more sacred than a ruffed grouse, a pheasant, or a mallard.

Pressure for a dove season persisted, but the opposition didn't let up.

Finally, it came to a vote at the spring fish and wildlife hearings held annually in every Wisconsin county. Attendance at the hearings is often sparse, but now opponents of the hunt turned out in numbers. Even more proponents were there. Many of them saw opposition to a dove hunt as an attack on all hunting. "What's next?" they wondered.

Backed by the support shown at the hearings, the Natural Resources Board approved a dove season. Legal challenges followed but failed, and in 2003, Wisconsin had its first modern-day mourning dove hunt.

What has it done to the dove population? Nothing noticeable. Wisconsin hunters don't turn out for the dove hunt the way they do for the deer season. And this bird is not as easy a target as you might think from seeing it perched on a telephone wire. According to one study, it takes eight shotgun shells, on average, to bring down a single dove.

The Wisconsin dove population remains stable.

The Prairie Chicken

Indian tribes are said to have modeled ceremonial dances on the mating display of the prairie chicken. Quite a display it is.

The birds perform in spring in mating areas, called leks. The males inflate orange air sacs on their necks, make a loud cooing sound called booming, and engage in brief fights with other males that intrude on their territory. Meanwhile, hens watch with feigned indifference.

In the early days of white settlement, the birds were found in the prairies and savannas of Southern Wisconsin. After the northern forest was cut and burned, they spread and, for a time, were found in every county. But if nature truly abhors a vacuum, it also has a grudge against open land if it's capable of growing trees.

As the northern forest regenerated, and as agriculture took over the fertile land farther to the south, the prairie chicken population dwindled and now the bird is found only in scattered locations in Central Wisconsin. The principal stronghold is the Buena Vista Marsh in southern Portage County.

There, and in a few other locations, grasslands survive, and grass is what prairie chickens need for nesting habitat.

The prairie chicken is a grouse, a bird that resembles a chicken in many ways. Wisconsin has four grouse species:

–The spruce grouse, a bird of deep forests, so tame it has been nicknamed the fool hen. In Wisconsin, it's found only in the far north.

–The ruffed grouse, an inhabitant of mixed forests in much of the state.

–The sharp-tailed grouse, a bird found mainly in brushy areas.

–And the prairie chicken, a grassland bird. It has several sub-species. The one found in Wisconsin is the greater prairie chicken.

All except the ruffed grouse, a popular game bird, are in trouble today in Wisconsin.

The Buena Vista Marsh, which has the best population of prairie chickens, is a drained wetland. To keep it suitable for the birds, thousands of acres have been bought and maintained in grass by such techniques as controlled burns.

Frederick and Fran Hamerstrom, biologists for the Wisconsin Conservation Department, now the Department of Natural Resources, developed a strategy for preventing the disappearance of the prairie chicken from the state. Their plan called for acquiring scattered 40-acre plots on the marsh and keeping them in grass.

Selling the idea to people on the marsh proved extraordinarily difficult, as described by Fran Hamerstrom in her book, *Strictly for the Chickens*. As she told it, a local politician claimed the prairie chicken's problems were caused by foxes and snowy owls, arctic birds that often winter on the marsh.

Fred Hamerstrom, Fran's husband, argued that the birds had co-existed with predators from time immemorial, and what they needed was good nesting cover.

The local politician, wrote Fran, made quite a bit of money trapping foxes for bounties and was irritated by Fred's argument. The word got around that the Hamerstroms wanted the state to buy the whole marsh. A petition was circulated and sent to the governor, the gist of which was that the goal should be to get rid of the foxes and the Hamerstroms.

The land purchase crisis was resolved when private foundations, rather than the state, stepped in and began buying property on the marsh, eventually acquiring acreage in the thousands and keeping it on the tax rolls. Paul Olson of Madison, a teacher, was one of the heroes in this effort. A wildlife area west of Stevens Point has been named for him.

Years later, one of the foundations sold its land to the state, over the opposition of town boards on the marsh because it would take it off the tax rolls. But by then, the Department of Natural Resources was making payments in lieu of taxes on land it owned, and the town boards discovered they weren't being hurt. A leading advocate of the prairie chicken, Sharon Schwab, was later elected chairperson of Grant, one of the towns on the marsh.

Habitat purchases are still being made and the DNR is keeping them in grass.

The prairie chicken was once a prime game bird, but it hasn't been a legal target in the state since the 1950s. Hunting wasn't the cause of the specie's decline, but it was felt the low population couldn't stand more pressure, although some DNR people, and the Hamerstroms too, thought a controlled hunt wouldn't be a problem.

Today, field trialers and their dogs still compete on the marsh, but only to find and flush the birds, not shoot them. And every spring, people crouch in blinds to watch the birds perform their mating dance.

A problem for the prairie chicken is lack of genetic diversity, caused by inbreeding and leading to low reproduction. The scattered populations are separated by forest regeneration and urban sprawl, and the birds no longer swap genes. To introduce new genes, prairie chickens were brought in for several years from Western Minnesota and released on the marsh.

A Comeback Story

I can't call myself a birder. I love seeing a bald eagle, knowing this majestic bird, once on the road to extinction in the lower 48 states, has made a remarkable comeback. But I have trouble telling one species of sparrow from another, though I'm pretty good at differentiating cardinals and blue jays.

I got a kick some years ago at witnessing the annual sandhill crane gathering on the Platte River near Kearney, Nebraska. They were mostly lesser sandhills, a little smaller bird than the greater sandhills we have in Wisconsin. The lesser sandhills mainly winter in the southwestern states and Mexico, while nesting in northern Canada and Alaska. Some continue on over the Bering Strait, deep into Siberia.

On the way north, they stop on the Platte and refuel, feeding on waste corn left over from the previous fall's harvest. As many as half a million gather there before moving on. We don't have anything quite like that in Wisconsin, but greater sandhills do congregate in the fall before heading south. One place where they gather by the thousands is the Sandhill State Wildlife Area near Babcock. By the way, the wildlife area is named for sandy ridges on the property, not the bird.

Once nearly extirpated in Wisconsin, the sandhill, like the bald eagle, has bounced back. It has recovered to the point where people are talking of a crane hunting season, like they have in states west of us.

Would this reduce a problem cranes cause for farmers? When corn germinates, cranes sometimes go down the rows, pull up the sprouts, and eat the kernels. Propane exploders scare them away, but only briefly. Some people think they'd stay away longer if they'd been shot at a few times by hunters. Not everyone agrees.

A crane season might be difficult for people, even some hunters, to accept, just as the mourning dove season was.

But, as in the case of the dove hunt, there's no biological reason not to have a crane hunt as long as it's tightly controlled. It's just that it would be difficult to get used to shooting a bird that once was on the verge of disappearing from the state.

Let's hope it doesn't turn into another mourning dove battle where people ask, "What do you want to hunt next, robins?"

Bluebirds

The bluebirds of happiness have reasons to be even happier now that the Aldo Leopold Audubon Society is on their case. The Central Wisconsin organization has developed a bluebird trail with more than a thousand nesting boxes.

In 10 years, the trail produced thousands of bluebirds and other cavity nesting bird species—wrens, chickadees, and tree swallows.

The bluebird has experienced a lot of troubles, and in the 40 years preceding the 1980s, its numbers declined 90%. A large part of this was due to the disappearance of hollow trees and wooden fence posts in which the species nested.

Erection of nesting boxes was part of the solution. Another part has been monitoring the boxes and kicking out unwanted intruders like house sparrows.

Successful monitoring requires dedicated volunteers, and the society has them. The volunteers also built and erected the nesting boxes. The society's trail is thought to be the longest in North America and, for two years in a row, produced the most bluebirds of any trail in Wisconsin.

I'm not one of the volunteers, and my sole contribution to the bluebird recovery was the installation of a single successful nesting box. I put it up on the edge of a pine plantation I own.

I didn't think it was a good spot. However, it seemed to be the best place I had, and when I went by it a couple of weeks later, a bird with a bright blue back and a reddish breast was perched on the box. A male bluebird. He and his mate brought off a successful hatch and its been repeated most years since.

Bluebird nesting boxes don't have to be fancy, but the proper dimensions and the right size of the entry hole help. Also, these birds aren't colony nesters, so the right spacing between boxes is important.

Even before the Aldo Leopold Audubon Society got into the act, people were coming to the rescue of the bluebird. Herman Olson, a retired U.S. Forest Service employee, made at least 700 nesting boxes with the help of volunteers and sold them at cost.

The boxes sometimes attract critters other than birds, such as deer mice. A nesting box I put up elsewhere on my tree plantation attracted a flying squirrel. It was a surprise to open the box and see a bug-eyed animal staring out at me. I decided it was welcome to stay.

The Rising Star Mill on the Tomorrow River

Rivers

Our Namesake River

In Wisconsin, we like to brag about our 14,000 lakes (or is it 15,000?).

We should also be boasting of our rivers—the Mississippi on the western border, the Wolf, the Fox, the Chippewa, the St. Croix and the Brule, and thousands of miles of trout streams. And of course, the Wisconsin River, which makes a 420-mile run from Lac Vieux Desert on the Michigan line down to the Mississippi.

The Wisconsin River is part of our history. It was a highway for Indians and early settlers, a transportation route for loggers, and a power source for electric utilities.

It was also an open sewer, but because of the federal Clean Water Act of 1972, it's vastly improved. It's an incomparable asset and cities have taken advantage of it with dramatic improvements to their riverfronts.

Give the credit to the Clean Water Act, to the Wisconsin Department of Natural Resources for implementing it, and to Bob Martini of Rhinelander for expertly supervising the operation for the DNR.

The river always had fish even when badly polluted, but they tasted bad, especially downstream from paper mills. Now it has more fish and a greater variety, and they're edible. The channel catfish and white bass are newcomers to the upper river. Lake sturgeon were eradicated long ago, except on the lower Wisconsin, but are being reintroduced by the DNR. Smallmouth bass and walleyes are abundant and muskies are more common.

The Wisconsin River drains some 12,000 square miles, almost a quarter of the state's area, and has a drop of more than 1,050 feet from source to mouth (from the pinnacle atop the Empire State Building to the ground is 1,453 feet). The river has 26 dams, but none below Prairie du Sac. The last 92-mile stretch down to the Mississippi was designated in 1989 as the Lower Wisconsin River Waterway and is being preserved in an unspoiled state. The part above that isn't pristine, but it's still a good river.

Is the Wisconsin River perfect? Not really. It still gets more toxic discharges than other state rivers. That's because it's big and long and has a lot of cities and industries on its banks. A couple of the river's impoundments have algae blooms caused by phosphorus runoff.

So, though the river is much improved, it could be better. But it's not like it was in 1948 when *Electrical World*, a trade publication, said the river "does a sewage disposal job which, under other conditions, would require many expensive sewage disposal plants." In other words, it was all right to pollute the Wisconsin with raw sewage if it saved money. We think differently now.

What does the word "Wisconsin" mean?

Very simple. In an Indian language, it means "gathering of the waters." Unless it means "grassy place." Or perhaps "river that meanders through something red," possibly a reference to the red stone bluffs at Wisconsin Dells. Unless the "red" is the pinkish rock found at Stevens Point and Wisconsin Rapids. Or maybe the word means "Stream of a Thousand Isles," "muskrat house," or even "holes in the bank of a stream, in which birds nest."

Whatever its meaning, the word came from the Chippewa tongue. Unless it came from the Miami tribe's language. Or possibly it's a corruption of a French word.

Early historians interviewed elderly Indians, French residents, and fur traders about the meaning of "Wisconsin," and one of them said, "I have not found two Indians to agree on the meaning of this word."

So now you know what Wisconsin means. How did the river get its name? It started with Father Jacques Marquette, the French-Canadian priest who paddled down the river in 1673 on his voyage from Lake Michigan to the Mississippi and downstream. He called it the "Miscousing." His companion, Louis Joliet, spelled it "Miskonsing."

Another French-Canadian explorer, La Salle, misread Marquette's handwriting and came up with "Ouisconsing." Others garbled it even more and turned it into "Ouisconsin," and this was the spelling usually used well into the 19th century. Then it was Americanized to "Wisconsin," though a territorial governor, James Doty, wanted it spelled "Wiskonsan." Finally, the state Legislature nailed down the spelling we use today.

One more thing, and this is something on which the experts agree: The Wisconsin River wasn't named after the state of Wisconsin. The state of Wisconsin was named after the Wisconsin River.

Dam Facts

Often, one of the first things people did when arriving in unsettled country was build a dam on the nearest stream. The dams powered sawmills and grist mills, and frequently a community grew around them. Later, some of them became generators of electricity.

But the days of dam construction appear to have ended in Wisconsin. The good sites have been developed and attitudes have changed. Dams with no economic purpose are being gradually removed.

That's a switch. A 1948 booklet put out by *Electrical World* said "great possibilities remain" in terms of new dams on the Wisconsin River and its tributaries. That was when the biggest water project in the state's history was being planned but didn't quite become reality. Michael Goc wrote about it in his book, *Stewards of the Wisconsin*.

The project was planned by the Wisconsin Valley Improvement Co. (WVIC) and Consolidated Water Power & Paper Co. It called for a dam on the Big Eau Pleine River in Marathon County, near where it joins the Wisconsin, creating a 7,000-acre reservoir. Also, there'd be a dam on the nearby Little Eau Pleine River, creating a 45,000-acre (70 square mile) reservoir, the biggest inland water body in the state, next to Lake Winnebago.

Normal runoff wouldn't have filled the reservoirs. So the plan called for a canal, 6 miles long and 80 feet wide, from above the Mosinee dam down the west side of the Wisconsin River to the Big Eau Pleine, to fill that reservoir with spring flood waters. Then a 2,800-foot-long tunnel, 30 feet in diameter, would have taken water from the Big Eau Pleine to the Little Eau Pleine to fill that impoundment.

This would have greatly increased the Wisconsin River Valley's water storage. To make full use of the power potential, hydro-electric dams were proposed at Petenwell and Castle Rock, downstream from Wisconsin Rapids. Still another twist was an enlargement of the canal at Portage to take Wisconsin River water to the Fox River, increasing hydroelectric generation at dams between Lake Winnebago and Green Bay.

The planning began during the Great Depression of the 1930s, when the federal government was pouring money into public works projects. Consolidated and WVIC sought some of it, but instead, the funds went for things like schools and sewage treatment plants.

However, the WVIC-Consolidated project wasn't quite dead. The Big Eau Pleine Reservoir and the Castle Rock and Petenwell hydro dams were built, but not the canal to the Big Eau Pleine, the pipe to the Little Eau Pleine, or the diversion to the Fox River.

As for the huge Little Eau Pleine Reservoir, problems with roads, rising costs, and objections from conservationists created obstacles. And times were changing. The use of electricity was soaring, and it became apparent that hydropower couldn't begin to meet the demand in Wisconsin. That's still true. I believe hydro generates only about 5% of the state's electricity today, and only about 7% of the nation's.

First WVIC and then Consolidated took note of reality and dropped out of the Little Eau Pleine project, and in 1959, Consolidated donated the 20,000 acres it owned there to the state. Now it is the George W. Mead State Wildlife Area, one of Wisconsin's treasured outdoor resources.

On the national level, another blow to dam construction came in the 1970s with the Tellico dam in Tennessee. Critics argued that the dam could cause the extinction of the snail darter, an obscure little fish. The snail darter became the object of ridicule, with dam proponents arguing that it was insignificant and shouldn't hold up a beneficial project.

The extinction of any species is no small matter, and aside from that, a lot more was at stake than the fish. The reservoir behind the dam would displace farms, villages, and people, and the project had questionable economic value. Tellico was built, but the controversy helped make further dam construction unpopular.

Another dam that didn't happen was one proposed in the 1950s on the New Wood River in Wisconsin's Lincoln County. This one would have flooded land bought by the state for winter deer yards. Among the opponents were the Wisconsin Conservation Department and the Wisconsin Federation of Conservation Clubs, represented by its secretary, Les Woerpel of Stevens Point, who had also been a foe of the Little Eau Pleine Reservoir.

Few people will argue that dams are all bad. They generate clean, renewable energy and hold back potential flood water. The Chippewa, Willow, Turtle-Flambeau, and Rainbow Flowages in Northern Wisconsin are important fish and wildlife resources. But it's safe to say no more dams will be built in the Wisconsin River watershed, though proposed projects keep popping up out west and in other countries.

American Rivers, a national river advocacy organization, says many dams have outlived their usefulness. "Communities that choose to pull out obsolete dams," said the organization, "can benefit from better water quality, revitalized fisheries, new recreational opportunities, increased real estate values, and recovered land suitable for parks and other public use."

Since 1967, about a hundred dams have been taken out in Wisconsin.

Little Plover

It could be called a poster child for water conservation or a canary in the mine shaft, warning us of what might happen if we don't take care of our water resources.

The Little Plover River is where many fishermen caught their first trout. It's hurting, but not dead, and work is under way to restore it to at least partial health. The problem is groundwater withdrawals. In other words, heavy pumping for irrigated agriculture and municipal purposes is draining the river's water source.

The Department of Natural Resources prepared a master plan for the Little Plover Fishery Area in 1985, and even then the stream had problems. The plan said the trout population had crashed, and the suspected cause was agricultural chemicals. It may have been a crop duster's overspray.

The master plan pointed to other threats, increasing groundwater pumping and residential encroachment. It warned that up to 90% of the stream's flow could be depleted in time by drought and pumping. That was an underestimate. A section of the stream dried up entirely in several recent summers. It wasn't a total surprise. Professor George Kraft, a hydrologist at the University of Wisconsin-Stevens Point, had forecast to the year when it would happen. To further validate the predictions in the master plan, there's been a big residential build-up in the watershed.

Few trout streams have been studied as thoroughly as the Little Plover. The U.S. Geological Survey, the Wisconsin Conservation Department, and its successor, the Department of Natural Resources, have looked at it closely, starting in the 1960s. Early in the game, a Conservation Department official, Lewis Posekany, said he at first thought the Little Plover was just another trout stream, but learned it was a very good stream. That was true at the time.

The Little Plover is a miniature gem, only about five miles long from its source at the foot of the terminal moraine, where the glacier stopped, to the Wisconsin River.

The best part, from a fisherman's standpoint, was the 3.5 mile stretch from Springville Pond up to the source. The pond was created in the mid-1800s, when white settlement was new, to power a flour and grist mill. Above that, the Little Plover remained quite pristine, and for a long time it had a healthy trout population. Natural reproduction was sufficient.

However, the 1985 master plan said a recent survey had shown the stream had only 106 trout per acre of water, while surveys 15 or 20 years earlier had turned up populations of 1,800 to 2,900 per acre. The Little Plover is narrow, and it takes quite a bit of its surface to make an acre.

"It is believed that chemical contamination from agricultural sources" may have caused the decline, said the master plan. The stream recovered from that, only to be hit by the double whammy of urban sprawl and heavy groundwater pumping.

Long ago, men and boys flocked to the Little Plover on the opening day of trout season. An old-timer told me he used to ride to the stream on the handlebars of his father's bicycle.

The state created the Little Plover Fishery Area in 1957, and by 1985, the DNR owned 254 acres out of a goal of 381 acres. In the master plan, it was predicted, correctly, that further acquisitions would be difficult because of competition from land developers.

Over the years, efforts were made to improve trout habitat in the stream, but it no longer is a magnet for fishermen. So is the Little Plover a dead issue?

It's hard to imagine it again being a premier trout stream as long as heavy groundwater pumping continues. No one set out to harm the Little Plover, but with no controls on high capacity wells, it happened and will be hard to undo. Irrigators and the village of Plover have a big investment in their wells, and aren't likely to quit pumping soon.

But the stream is getting help. A citizens' organization, Friends of the Little Plover River, has been formed to advocate for it.

There's a Little Plover River Work Group made up of representatives of state, county, and local governments and university and private groups, including potato and vegetable growers. This led to the establishment of a public rights stage, below which the stream's flow is not supposed to drop except in a drought.

The village of Plover is buying land in the watershed and taking it out of irrigation. The money for the purchase is coming from Portage County's Land Preservation Fund and the state Stewardship program. And the village now pumps 85% of its water from a well two miles from the Little Plover instead of from two wells a half-mile from the water. Others are also taking steps to reduce groundwater pumping.

Tighter state laws controlling groundwater pumping have been proposed, but not passed. Dan Mahoney, Plover's village administrator, believes locally led efforts have to come first.

Despite it all, the Little Plover River Fishery Area continues to be an island of nature in an urbanizing community. The 1985 master plan said, "In future years, as human populations increase and wild lands shrink, residents will treasure the naturalness of this area and look forward to enjoying the recreational and educational use of the wildlife it will harbor."

A good trout population on top of that would be a bonus.

Tomorrow

Vern Hacker, a Department of Natural Resources fish biologist, once told me the Tomorrow River would be the top trout stream in Wisconsin, other than the Bois Brule, if the dams and mill ponds at Nelsonville and Amherst were removed. Later, he changed his mind and said it would be the best.

The Nelsonville dam is gone but the one at Amherst is still there. Al Niebur, another DNR fish biologist, said it gives the stream a temperature bump that affects it all the way down to the city of Waupaca. Trout, being cold water fish, don't like that. Also the dam blocks the movement of trout to and from upstream spawning grounds.

Don't get me started on whether the Amherst dam should come out. It's a community landmark and a community decision. I suspect it will remain unless and until defects in the structure threaten a big repair bill.

Even with the dam in place, the Tomorrow is quite a stream. It starts in northern Portage County and flows into Waupaca County, where it's called the Waupaca River. In his Portage County history, Malcolm Rosholt wrote that the river takes its name from the Menominee Indian words "Waubuch se-pee," meaning "Tomorrow River" or "river of pale water."

Like a lot of other translations of Indian words, this one is open to question. Rosholt also wrote, "Whether this is a Menominee word or not, the Chippewa word for the idea of 'tomorrow' is 'warbunk.'"

In the early 1970s, the stream was the scene of a controversial carp removal project. The Nelsonville and Amherst ponds were infested with carp and the Wisconsin DNR proposed to eliminate them with antimycin, a fish toxicant. It was a big project, involving about 50 miles of stream plus tributaries and a few connected lakes. It had considerable support from the public.

Critics noted that antimycin would kill all fish, not just carp. The Tomorrow had a rich fish fauna, some of it rare.

The DNR said it would remove trout and other species from the Tomorrow before putting in the antimycin, and would return them after the toxin was gone. And the agency contended antimycin was a natural compound and would have no lingering effects on the environment.

Legal efforts to block the project failed, and it proceeded in 1971. Once the antimycin was out of the Tomorrow, the DNR put back the fish it had removed. It also stocked the stream with hatchery trout.

When the season reopened the following spring, anglers said fishing had improved. Skeptics said that was because of heavy stocking.

The ironic thing is that proponents and opponents weren't all that far apart. They agreed that the Tomorrow's real problem was the two mill ponds. The DNR's Vern Hacker, I believe, didn't think either dam would come out in the foreseeable future.

He was thrilled when the Nelsonville dam and pond were bought by the DNR in 1984 and later removed. It happened because Barney Koziczkowski, the owner of the dam, wanted to retire. The dam provided power for his mill, where he ground grain. He wanted to sell it to someone who would keep on operating it but could find no buyer other than the DNR.

Most of the people in Nelsonville weren't happy and expressed their opposition at a meeting. But I remember Bob Bartig, the village president, telling them Barney wanted to retire and had no other buyer, and the village shouldn't stand in his way.

So the DNR bought it, removed the dam, and sold Koziczkowki's picturesque Rising Star Mill to the Portage County Historical Society for $1, and now it's operated as a museum and a place for concerts and art shows. With the water gone, the pond bed turned into a mud flat. But the Tomorrow re-established its old channel and the pond bottom soon greened up.

Harry's Dam

Christensen's dam is no more. It was on the Plover River, above Portage County's Jordan Park, and it was once known as Van Order's. The names of dams, and the mills they powered, often changed with the owner.

Harry Christensen used the dam to generate electricity, enough for his house across the road and for his shop, where he repaired machinery, but not enough to light up a city. The dam had only a seven and a half foot head.

The dam was picturesque, sort of a calendar scene. Earlier in its long history, the dam, or the ones preceding it, had powered a saw mill, a shingle mill, a grist mill, and a feed mill. The first dam at the site had probably been built in the 1850s.

Little dams like Harry's were important in the logging days. Big white pine grew along the Plover, which starts in Langlade County and runs through Marathon and Portage Counties before joining the Wisconsin River. The logs were sawed into lumber at mills along the stream, and the dams provided the power.

Millions of board, feet of logs, and lumber rafts floated down the Plover River, and early dams had slides so the rafts could go over.

Christensen's dam was a ramshackle affair and Harry had to keep repairing the damage caused by ice. He had bought it in 1942. Earlier in his life, which began in Rib Lake, he had, among other things, worked in a machine shop, was a tool and die maker, and once ran a filling station.

"As a kid I was what you call a rolling stone," said the peppery and outspoken Harry. "A rolling stone gathers no moss but gets a pretty good polish."

Harry died in 1985. There was no buyer for the dam, and in its condition, it probably was a menace to anything downstream, so it was removed and the Plover River runs free in that stretch. It's rocky from the old dam site downstream, making it challenging for canoeists and kayakers.

Mill Creek

Almost every Wisconsin stream, it seems, once had a sawmill or grist mill on its banks, and that's why we have so many Mill Creeks. They're about as numerous as Rocky Runs.

The Mill Creek I'm writing about, southwest of Stevens Point, apparently had several mills in the lumbering days, disappearing when the timber ran out.

The stream has a flow that's usually too high or too low for canoeing, seldom normal. It's a "flashy" creek—when it rains hard, there's a lot of runoff and Mill Creek is instantly at flood stage.

Its headwaters "spring" is the outfall pipe of the city of Marshfield's sewage treatment plant. Fortunately for Mill Creek's water quality, the treatment of sewage has improved, but this is still no trout stream. Never was, never will be. It's a warm water creek whose fish life, I believe, consists mostly of bullheads and minnows, although spawning walleyes and northern pike are known to have run upstream past Junction City.

I don't remember what induced the Klasinski brothers and me to canoe it. The day we did it was warm, the flow was low, the stream was shallow and rocky, and we did a lot of wading and portaging. It was scenic, running through a sort of rocky mini-canyon in one place, but

Rivers

that didn't quite make up for the downsides of the trip.

After a lot of paddling, dragging, and mosquito-swatting, we came to the end. Mercifully, a tavern was on Mill Creek's banks at our take-out point. We went in and had a cold beer, and maybe another.

I struck up a conversation with the bartender and asked him if anyone ever canoed down Mill Creek.

His answer was emphatic: "The devil himself couldn't come down that stream!"

Like hell he couldn't.

Mill Ponds

Mill ponds have a limited life expectancy. Every Wisconsin stream of any size had one, often several.

Communities grew up around them, and sometimes they were converted to electric power generators after the days of sawing lumber and grinding grain ended.

But in time, most of them had no economic function at all. Some of the ponds offered good fishing, but over time many silted in and became weedy. By then they had become community landmarks.

There's quite a story behind McDill Pond in Stevens Point. It's named for Dr. Alexander S. McDill (later a congressman) and his brother, Thomas H., early owners of the dam and of the mill associated with it. It was created by damming the Plover River in the early 1850s, and it successively powered a saw mill, a flouring mill, and a graphite mill. The graphite was mined north of Junction City and was used as a paint ingredient. The last economic use was as a pulp mill. This ended a few years after World War II.

The village of Whiting then bought the mill and the land downstream on the Plover and turned it into a park.

A double lynching in the 19th century had its roots in McDill Pond. The original owners of the dam that formed the pond were

Amos Courtwright and Luther Hanchett. Hanchett, like Alexander McDill, was later a congressman.

The mill was sold, and a dispute over a debt allegedly remaining from the sale led to a confrontation in 1875, in which the Portage County sheriff, Joseph Baker, was killed. The alleged killers, Amos Courtwright and his brother Isaiah, were dragged out of the county jail by a mob and hanged. No one was prosecuted for the lynching.

No such violence has been associated with the pond lately, but controversy has continued. In June 2011, a leak was discovered in the dam and the pond had to be drained. Although most of McDill Pond is in Stevens Point, with many homes built around it, the dam was still owned by the village of Whiting, which was unwilling to make the costly repairs.

Finally, the City of Stevens Point, Portage County, landowners on the pond, and the Department of Natural Resources agreed to put up the money.

Is the story over? As mentioned above, mill ponds have a limited life span. Sand washing in from upstream on the Plover River could make McDill Pond more shallow than it already is and necessitate dredging, which isn't cheap. Perhaps someday this will spark another controversy over who should pay for it.

A Cleaner River

When it comes to government regulations, there's plenty to gripe about. The government intrudes in our lives, telling us what we can't do and what we have to do. It makes things complicated, and we long for the days when bureaucrats weren't looking over our shoulders.

But think about it. Do you know what the Wisconsin River looked like (and smelled like) before the federal Clean Water Act of 1972? It had fish, but a lot fewer than today and they were barely edible, if that.

The problem was pollution from industries and municipalities. The Clean Water Act required paper mills, other industries, and communities to clean up their discharges.

The federal government mandated the work and the Department of Natural Resources managed it in Wisconsin. In the process, the DNR didn't win any popularity contests. Businesses and municipalities said they couldn't afford it, and a few industries hinted they'd move out of state. But because it was a federal law, they'd have faced a pollution abatement mandate wherever they went.

Municipalities weren't thrilled either, but they got government money to help them clean up.

In charge of the work on the Wisconsin River system was Bob

Martini of Rhinelander, who had earlier planned a career in medicine and wound up helping cure a sick stream. Earth Day celebrations in 1970 had induced him to change his plans and he joined the DNR, worked with the polluters, and got their cooperation.

Martini never claimed the river became as pristine as it was in pre-settlement days, but it's a heck of a lot cleaner. Parts of the Wisconsin have algae problems caused by things like run-off from farm fields and city streets, which in some ways are tougher to solve than industrial and municipal pollution. But solutions are being sought and will, in all likelihood, someday be found.

As for the clean-up's impact on the economy, no paper mills left the state as a result. The paper industry has problems, but they weren't caused by the Clean Water Act.

George Rogers atop Mt. Fuji

Adventure

Flambeau

The Flambeau River in Northern Wisconsin is a rapids-filled stream. It was a highway for Indians and voyageurs, a transporter of logs to sawmills during the lumbering heyday, and then became a challenging experience for canoeists and kayakers.

I paddled the north fork of the Flambeau twice, from Oxbo to Ladysmith.

The first time was in a group of six, two to a canoe. Four of us were just moderately experienced paddlers. The other two were more capable, or thought they were. They didn't worry much about the hazards of the Flambeau, not even Beaver Dam rapids, where a bronze marker was attached to a stone in memory of a man killed there. They even went down one rapid backwards and didn't tip.

Capsizing would have been no joke, since we were camping along the way. A night in a wet sleeping bag was not something to look forward to.

But we managed to keep our canoes upright all the way down to Little Falls, the last and most formidable obstacle on our three-day trip. Later, a dam was built and Little Falls was submerged by the reservoir it created. The dam generates some electricity, but not a lot. On the whole, I consider it a crime against nature, ruining one of

Adventure

the wildest and most scenic places on the river.

Little Falls was no Niagara, but it was a steep drop, and you could successfully canoe over it only if you were extra-careful. Our two canoeing experts went first; my companion and I and the other two canoeists followed a couple minutes later. It was a turbulent trip and we took water over the bow, but our canoes stayed upright. Below the falls, we saw some unusual things floating in the water—a hat, some camping gear, and one or two canoe paddles. Then we saw the experts, hauling the water-filled canoe up on shore.

We helped them retrieve what gear we could, though their fishing tackle went to the bottom of the Flambeau and stayed there.

We expressed our sympathy to our water-soaked companions with all the sincerity of the kindly waitresses who tell you to enjoy your meal, and the countless friendly people who urge you to have a nice day.

My second Flambeau trip was with Clint (Doc) Cragg, a veterinarian and a good canoeist. We camped along the way and remained upright and dry all the way down to Little Falls. Should we go over the falls? Sure, why not. I'd done it before and remembered some things from my previous visit to Little Falls, like the rocks to avoid. We made it without much trouble, though we took water over the bow. It was so much fun that we hauled the canoe upstream and ran the falls once more, again successfully. It was late in the season and I think we were the last two people ever to run the now-submerged Little Falls.

We continued on, fishing along the way but catching nothing. As we neared Ladysmith, we came upon a couple of fishermen in a rowboat, using cane poles. One of them threw his pole overboard and it began moving upstream against the current. He'd been using a big sucker for bait and a muskellunge had taken it. His strategy, maybe legal then, but not now, was for the musky to swallow the sucker, and with the hook in its intestines, it couldn't get away.

Doc shouted, "I'll give you $5 for that cane pole just as it lies in the water." Or maybe it was $10. Valuing money more than fish, the anglers agreed. We waited until the sucker had been swallowed. Doc,

149

the veterinarian, always carried a pistol to put a merciful end to any terminally ill cows he was treating. He picked up the cane pole, pulled the fish to the surface and shot it. It wasn't huge, but it was legal-sized.

Shooting fish was permitted at the time but was later outlawed, because bullets can ricochet off the water and hit unintended targets, like other fishermen. Doc gave the fisherman his money and his cane pole and we continued on our way.

At Ladysmith, we went into a tavern while waiting for our ride back to Oxbo, where we'd left our car, and I struck up a conversation with a woman at the bar. It turned out that her late husband had been a veterinarian long ago, just like Doc Cragg. Knowing something about conditions in the north in the old days, I asked her which he had treated most, animals or humans. "About equal," she said.

We continued on to Stevens Point, and all that was left was to concoct a thrilling story of how Doc had landed his monster musky after an epic battle.

Up Fuji

In Wisconsin, we don't get to climb mountains much, because there aren't any. Rib Mountain in Marathon County doesn't qualify. Its summit is just short of 2,000 feet above sea level, and it used to be called Rib Hill. That was before the tourism people got hold of it.

When we were college-age, Wayne McGown and I climbed the 555-foot-high Washington Monument. I'm not sure why. Maybe it was in tribute to the Father of Our Country. Or maybe, in the words of a famous mountaineer, "because it was there." Or maybe the elevator wasn't working that day.

Only once in my life have I climbed a real mountain. It was Fuji, that symmetrical snow-capped peak in Japan, where I happened to be on a taxpayer-financed trip (I was in the Army).

Fuji is a beautiful mountain, a symbol of Japan. Because it stands alone, not surrounded by other peaks, it's visible from afar. Some of us in our unit decided to climb it, just for the heck of it, I guess. Or maybe to test a saying that says, "He who comes to Japan and fails to climb Fuji is a fool, and he who climbs it twice is twice a fool."

Despite what you've heard, I'm not a fool. I climbed Fuji once and that was enough.

Ascending Fuji isn't traditional mountain-climbing, where you use ropes, pitons, and ice axes. It's a long hike uphill and thousands do it every summer when most of the snow is gone. People generally climb at night, when it's cooler.

We started in late afternoon. "We" being myself, Bill from Tennessee, Tom from Texas, Paul from Alabama, and a bunch of other GI's. At the outset, they gave us long wooden staffs, and at stations along the way, they burned something into them. It was in Japanese and I think it told how far we had climbed. I can't read Japanese, so I'm taking that on faith. Maybe the inscriptions really read "Yankee go home."

Some of the guys in our group dropped out along the way. Fuji may be a foothill by Himalayan standards, but our base was practically at sea level and the air became thinner as we climbed. Maybe the altitude got to them. Not far from the top, Tom sat down and said he couldn't go any farther. After a pep talk, he got up and made it the rest of the way.

We reached the top at dawn and expected to see a glorious panorama of the Japanese countryside laid out before us, with the Pacific Ocean in the distance. Not so. A solid cloud bank had formed below us and we saw only the tops of the clouds. A Japanese man who had climbed the mountain before (twice a fool?) was impressed, but I'd rather have seen the countryside.

Fuji is a volcano, not active but not extinct. It last erupted in 1707-08 and could do it again someday and cause another calamity for the Japanese, but probably not on the scale of the 2011 earthquake and tsunami. It has a huge crater, and when we were there, snow remained in it and someone was skiing.

We hiked down a different route from the one on which we'd come up, and along the way we found an airplane propeller, possibly a relic of World War II. From one of our planes or one of theirs? We couldn't tell.

At the peak of Fuji, they gave us pennants to attach to our staffs. On the pennant it says, "Top, 3776 meter" (12,388 feet). Not in a class with Mount Everest or many of the peaks in the Rockies, but a pretty good uphill hike. Strenuous enough to persuade me not to do it twice.

When my tour of duty in Japan ended, I wanted to bring the five-foot staff home, but it was too long to fit in a duffel bag. So I sawed it into four pieces and brought it that way. I reattached the pieces, and the staff is on a wall in our basement, a souvenir of my one and only mountain-climbing expedition.

A Perilous Trip

Whether or not they hunted or fished, the people who logged Wisconsin in the 19th century were outdoorsmen.

Lumberjacks worked in all kinds of weather. The story goes that one winter when the thermometer showed a temperature of 20 below zero, the men in one Wisconsin logging camp decided it was too cold to work. Their boss solved the problem by breaking the thermometer.

The crews on lumber rafts worked in spring and fall when river flows were high, and they too encountered chilly weather, compounded by wet clothes.

Until the coming of the railroads, rafts were the only practical way to get lumber to market. Logs would be floated to sawmills and cut up into planks, which were fastened into "cribs," 16 by 16 feet and 16 to 20 courses high. About seven of these, end to end, made a rapids piece, with a huge oar at the end for steering. Three rapids pieces, side by side, made a raft containing about one hundred thousand board feet of lumber. The river's current provided the propulsion.

"River craft approached these rafts at their peril," W.H. Glover wrote in an article in the 1941-42 *Wisconsin Magazine of History*.

Rafts were floated down the Wisconsin and Mississippi Rivers,

Adventure

usually to St. Louis, but sometimes farther. A "good trip" took about 24 days from Wausau to St. Louis.

It was a perilous voyage, over falls, rapids, and dams. Dams on the river were built with slides to allow the rafts to pass. Many raftsmen failed to survive. At Clint's Dam near present-day Wisconsin Rapids, 27 men were said to have drowned in a single season. And the shores of the river were strewn with wreckage long after rafting ended.

The worst of the natural obstacles were said to be Big Bull Falls at Wausau, Little Bull Falls at Mosinee, Conant's Rapids below Stevens Point, and Grand Rapids near Wisconsin Rapids.

River pilots guided the rafts downstream, and at really dangerous rapids, standing pilots took over. They were men with an especially good knowledge of this particular hazard. One of them, Isaac Ferris, is buried along the west side of the Wisconsin River below Stevens Point. He didn't drown. He died a natural death.

The lower Wisconsin River was less dangerous, but it had its hazards. A raft might blunder into a dead-end slough, and there was no way to back it out. Lumber salvaged from these rafts probably built many barns and houses in that part of the state.

Rafting was big business. At one point in the 1850s, a Stevens Point weekly newspaper, the *Wisconsin Pinery*, said both shores of the river were lined with rafts as far as the eye could see. The Wisconsin Central Railroad arrived in Stevens Point in 1871 and that was the beginning of the end for rafting, but not the end. The railroad couldn't handle all the lumber at first, and some lumbermen continued to use rafts for whatever reason.

The last lumber raft is said to have passed Stevens Point in 1883. By that time, lumber from the Wisconsin River watershed had helped build many cities west of the Mississippi River.

I had a grandfather who took rafts down to St. Louis. I wish I had been a little older before he died so I could have questioned him about it.

Photo courtesy of Sara Rebers
White Pine Needles

PLANTS

The Right Pine

I have a favorite tree, the white pine. It grows tall, makes great lumber, and looks impressive.

The loggers who came to Wisconsin in the 19th century found white pine up to 200 feet tall, each of which made an extreme amount of board feet at the sawmill.

The best way to get logs to the mill in those days was to float them there, since roads were primitive and logging railroads didn't go everywhere. Conveniently, the best white pines grew close to the shores of rivers and lakes, and the light wood floated well.

The Yawkey Lumber Co. had a sawmill at Hazelhurst on Lake Katherine, which had no natural connection to any other body of water. So the lumber company had a canal dug from Lake Katherine to Lake Tomahawk, ostensibly so logs could be floated in to the sawmill.

However, as the project neared completion, a problem was discovered: Lake Katherine was higher than Lake Tomahawk. A dam was placed at the end of the canal, which kept Lake Katherine from being lowered, but made it useless for floating logs to the mill.

That was the story, anyway. I had an uncle who was in charge of a lumber operation at Park Falls for many years and he didn't believe it. He said no lumberman was so dumb that he wouldn't have had a survey made before digging the canal, which would have shown the difference in the lakes' elevations.

The Yawkeys and their relatives had summer homes on Lake Katherine and my uncle was convinced the canal was dug for recreational purposes. A tram took boats over the dam and it gave access to Lake Tomahawk, a much bigger body of water, and to the whole Minocqua chain of lakes.

Back to the white pine. Not only is it a good-looking tree and a source of excellent lumber, it also grows fast. I have some in my yard that I planted when they were maybe 18 inches high and they're impressive now, big enough to attract the interest of a lumberman, if logging were permitted in town.

A downside of the white pine is its susceptibility to disease, including blister rust. The disease spreads from a white pine to a currant or gooseberry plant and then back to a white pine. So if you could get rid of all the currants and gooseberries, you'd eliminate blister ruse. That's pretty difficult, so we have to live with the disease to some extent.

Still, the white pine continues to do pretty well, and the state tree nurseries keep growing and selling it. Also, it reproduces prolifically. I own a piece of rural land where I planted red pine years ago. It's been logged several times and now young trees are coming up on the forest floor. Most of them are white pines, the offspring of mother trees on the edge of the property.

Not a bad deal, in my opinion. My woodland is being taken over by a better tree and it isn't costing me a nickel. Nature is doing it for me, for free.

Not Just a Crazy Weed

Locoweed is a combination of two words: loco, meaning crazy, and weed, meaning an unwanted plant, often a pest.

Locoweed plants out West cause a nervous disorder when eaten by livestock, but Fassett's locoweed is non-toxic. It grows in Portage, Waushara, Bayfield, and Douglas Counties in Wisconsin and nowhere else, and is on the federal endangered plant list.

In Portage County, it grows along Pickerel Lake in the southeastern corner. It apparently came down ahead of the glacier and resembles a plant that grows in the Arctic. During the Ice Age, Wisconsin was a treeless tundra and the plant was probably common. When the glacier retreated, other plants moved in and outcompeted Fassett's locoweed in most locations.

It survived only on the shores of a few hard-water lakes with fluctuating water levels. When the water level is down and the sandy lake bed is exposed, locoweed seeds sprout, and locoweed grows well in the absence of competition. Eventually other plants move in and crowd the locoweed, but by that time it has dropped its seeds on the former lake bed.

When precipitation increases and the lake rises, it drowns out all the terrestrial plants. But the locoweed seed remains viable, and it sprouts when the water level drops. This is a routine that's been going on for thousands of years.

The plant is a foot tall, or maybe a little less, and has an attractive blossom. It's named for Norman Fassett, the University of Wisconsin-Madison taxonomist who first identified it and who played a leading role in establishing Wisconsin's natural areas system. Appropriately, one of those state natural areas is on the shore of Pickerel Lake.

The plant was found at the lake in 1963, and Robert Freckmann, a now retired botany professor at the University of Wisconsin-Stevens Point, is credited with calling attention to it.

Similar plants grow elsewhere in the northern hemisphere, but Fassett's locoweed is slightly different.

What good is Fassett's locoweed? Some years ago, Freckmann said, "I wish people wouldn't ask that question." "A species shouldn't have to justify its existence," he said, although he noted that rare plants may contain things such as medicines that benefit humans.

In an effort to guarantee its survival, the state Department of Natural Resources has bought land on which Fassett's locoweed grows. It owns three-fourths of the frontage on Pickerel Lake.

Forest Primeval

Since photography was not far advanced in those days, we owe our mental picture of Wisconsin's primeval Northwoods to the field notes of pioneer surveyors and descriptions by early geologists.

John T. Curtis, of the University of Wisconsin-Madison, was the author of *The Vegetation of Wisconsin,* published in 1959, and he based much of his information on the records left by those geologists and surveyors. Curtis wrote that "by no means all of Northern Wisconsin was covered by a dense carpet of virgin forest." Instead, "barrens, park-like areas of scattered and stunted trees, and stretches of thin forest of small pine, oak, and aspen were mixed with widely spaced patches or larger tracts of mature forest."

Curtis told about a trip geologist J.G. Norwood took in 1847 from La Pointe on Madeline Island in Lake Superior, overland to the Wisconsin River and then down to Prairie du Chien. Norwood wrote, "In general, the flat or gently rolling uplands were sparsely timbered, while the heavy forests were restricted to the deeper valleys."

Just north of Stevens Point, the west side of the river supported "a small growth of oak, elm, and aspen, while east of the river a beautiful undulating prairie extends as far as the eye can reach." North of Wisconsin Rapids, "The country is a rolling sand plain with a few pine bushes and dwarf oaks scattered over it."

In Northern Wisconsin, Curtis wrote, pine grew on uplands—jack and red pine on lighter sands, and white pine on sandy loam. On heavier soil, the trees were a mixture of white pine, hemlock, balsam, white spruce, sugar maple, basswood, yellow birch, beech, elm, red oak, and ironwood.

The purpose of the government survey that supplied much of Curtis' information was to establish boundary lines so land could be sold to settlers, but the surveyors recorded other data, too. Traveling through swamps and forests, far from any towns, without such things as geographic positioning systems, must have been a man-killing job. No doubt the surveyors made mistakes. It was a miracle they didn't make more.

How difficult was it? *Wisconsin Natural Resources* magazine, in its August 2009 issue, printed an excerpt from a letter written in 1847 by government surveyor H.A. Wiltsie. For four consecutive weeks, he wrote, no one in his surveying crew had dry clothes, and they were tormented by clouds of mosquitoes and other insects while they worked and camped in the wild. Wiltsie was paid to do it, and he said he had "a great fondness for camp life," but he also said he wouldn't do it again no matter what they paid him.

One surveyor, who achieved a measure of fame, was Joshua Hathaway, who in 1839-40 led the government survey of a three-mile-wide strip on both banks of the Wisconsin River from Nekoosa up past Stevens Point and north to the Big Eau Claire River in Marathon County. This was land that had just been ceded to the government by the Menominee tribe.

In his Portage County history, Malcolm Rosholt wrote that Hathaway was a Revolutionary War veteran who served with Ethan Allen's Green Mountain Boys. He said Hathaway had graduated from Yale and helped break ground for the Erie Canal before coming west.

Rosholt's history is priceless, but all historians make an occasional mistake, and Malcolm made one here. He had the surveyor, Hathaway, confused with another Joshua Hathaway, possibly his father. The younger Hathaway was born in 1810, long after the Revolutionary War ended.

Rosholt said a Hathaway portrait is among the paintings in the collection of the State Historical Society in Madison. That's the younger Hathaway's portrait, I'm sure.

The Juniper-Bird Link

A red cedar tree, also known as juniper, sprouted in our yard a couple of years ago. I didn't plant it. I think a bird did.

The red cedar, not a close relative of the white cedar, is common in Southern Wisconsin and states to the south, like Illinois and Kentucky. It sprouts on almost any soil: in abandoned farm fields, along roadsides, or in any other sunny location. It has an attractive conical shape.

Above a line across the middle of Wisconsin, it's scarce, perhaps because it's a little too cold in the north. That may change.

A downside of the red cedar is that it tends to take over a field. Not so good if you want it to stay open for grassland, plants, and animals. The tree is an early stage in forest succession, and in time is replaced by other species.

The red cedar is medium-sized and has reddish wood. It's aromatic and moths don't like it, so it's used to line clothes, closets, and make cedar chests.

I was in the Army at Fort Knox, Kentucky. While on bivouac, I picked up a piece of red cedar wood. With nothing much else to do, I started whittling on it with a jack knife. I didn't finish the job until I got out of the Army, when I turned it into a big spoon.

I gave it to our daughter Jane, now living in Portland, Oregon, and

I think she still has it. I'll have to ask.

Now, about the bird I think planted the juniper in our yard. Red cedar seeds are in berries—which are actually small, modified cones. Birds like to eat the berry. They digest most of it but not the seed. In the digestion process, the seed gets an acid bath, which breaks down its dormancy. Eventually the bird excretes the seed along with a dash of fertilizer, and presto, a red cedar tree.

I've been told a red cedar seed won't sprout without that acid bath. So here we have a bird and a tree cooperating unconsciously. The bird gets something to eat and the tree gets help in reproducing. They call it synergy—two or more things functioning together to produce a result not independently available.

Big Trees

I have a liking for big trees, and I wish the old-time Wisconsin lumbermen had left a few more. The state had white pines topping 200 feet, but they were harvested at a time when clearing the forests for agriculture was the thing to do. Some of my ancestors were among those responsible.

Of course the whole state wasn't covered with big pines. You might get that impression from 19th century photos of huge logs on sleighs, heading for the sawmill. But in his book, *Lumbermen on the Chippewa*, Malcolm Rosholt wrote that the logs were usually chosen for the benefit of the cameraman, "an early form of boosterism."

Although I love old-growth forests, second-growth isn't all bad. Few deer or ruffed grouse are found in virgin timber, but they thrive in the forest that grew up after the big ones were cut. However, some wildlife is found only in old-growth. For the most part they may not be the kind we hunt, but that doesn't mean they're unimportant. We need both kinds of forest.

We never had trees the size of those on the West Coast, but no one else did either. Douglas firs grow to a monstrous size out there, and I've seen trucks in Oregon carrying only three logs because there wasn't room for more.

Sequoias and redwoods get even larger. The tallest is the redwood. A redwood named "Hyperion," for a Titan god in Greek mythology, was discovered in 2006, and at 379.3 feet, it's considered the tallest in the world. Another source lists it as 379.1 feet, but who's to argue over a couple inches? The estimated wood content of this tree is 18,600 cubic feet and its estimated age is 700 to 800 years.

The tree was discovered in a remote part of Redwood National Park in Northern California. The exact location hasn't been revealed for fear that human traffic would upset the surrounding ecosystem. It's possible an even taller redwood might be found if someone bothered to look.

Though not as tall as redwoods, related sequoia trees are even older—thousands of years—and even bulkier.

And even the sequoia doesn't reach the age of the bristlecone pine. One, in Nevada's Great Basin National Park, is more than 4,800 years old. It lives about two miles above sea level and reached this great age in spite of (or more likely because of) the fact that it has been stunted by cold and drought. It's not a tree of soaring beauty.

Now it faces a double threat. One is blister rust, a disease brought over from Europe a century ago, which also affects our white pines. We've had it in a couple of trees in our yard. The other threat is the pine bark beetle, an insect pest in the high-elevation West, aggravated by warming temperatures.

I've seen redwoods and sequoias and was awed. Redwoods like a mild climate and have been grown in England and New Zealand, but wouldn't make it here. But I thought the sequoia might survive, as it grows under colder conditions than the redwood. Once, in Yosemite National Park, we were unable to get into one of the sequoia groves because the snow was too deep. And that was in June.

In another sequoia grove, I picked up some cones, shook out the seeds, and planted them in our yard. They sprouted but didn't survive. Come to think of it, an enormous sequoia would probably be in the way a couple thousand years from now.

Wisconsin Cactus

Wisconsin has well over 600 state natural areas, protecting outstanding natural communities, geological formations, and archeological sites. They're the last refuges in the state for some rare plants and animals.

Among the oddball plants growing in two of them (oddball for Wisconsin, anyway) are a couple varieties of cactus. Aren't cacti desert plants and isn't this a pretty moist state? Right on both counts, but we still have cactus, though not the saguaros you'll find in Arizona.

Prickly pear cacti grow in Southwestern Wisconsin, notably in the Spring Green Preserve. It's a sandy area, created by an outwash of the lower Wisconsin River, and it's sometimes called the Wisconsin Desert. The preserve has other plants not ordinarily found in this part of the country.

A smaller variety of the prickly pear grows on Poppy's Rock, also known as Cactus Rock, a stone outcropping in eastern Waupaca County, not far from New London. I believe it's Wisconsin's northernmost cactus.

Although designated as state natural areas, neither the Spring Green Preserve nor Poppy's Rock is state-owned. The Spring Green Preserve belongs to the Nature Conservancy and Poppy's Rock is owned by Lawrence University.

Quite a few plant species are in trouble in the state because of things like land development and browsing by deer. Most of these plants are obscure and have no value to humans as far as we know. But you can't be sure, and natural areas help protect them.

The foxglove plant was long used in Europe as a treatment for heart trouble and its users thought it helped them. It did. Digitalis, still a useful heart remedy, is derived from the foxglove. Other plants have also been found to have medicinal uses, though the surface has just been scratched.

Even those plants that don't wind up in the pharmacy may have values we don't recognize. And if they're not protected, we never will know.

The Scrub Pine

The jack pine isn't my favorite yard tree. Probably not yours either. The wood contains a lot of fiber and makes good paper. As lumber, however, it's not in a class with black walnut, red oak, or white pine. And it's not a thing of beauty, especially when it grows in the open with no other trees around it. Then it develops scraggly limbs and resembles an octopus.

Maybe you could call it a scrub pine. But it grows on dry, sandy soil where little else thrives, and it heals the land after forest fires. Recognizing its value, the Wisconsin Department of Natural Resources continues to grow jack pine seedlings in its tree nurseries for sale to the public.

Jack pines are stingy with their seeds. Some of their cones stay closed for years, opening only after a hot fire. Then they shower their seeds on the burnt soil and a jack pine forest develops.

A jack pine woods doesn't look like good wildlife habitat, but it's important for the survival of a rare bird, Kirtland's warbler. In its stronghold, the lower peninsula of Michigan, the bird nests only under jack pines 5 to 20 feet tall.

At one time, lower Michigan was the only place where it nested, but now it has spread to Michigan's upper peninsula, Ontario, and

Wisconsin. In Wisconsin, it has been found nesting under red pines as well as jacks.

Wisconsin is at the south edge of the jack pine range, which extends well up into Canada. The tree is similar to the lodgepole pine of the West, and where the species meet, they're said to hybridize.

Almost all the trees in our yard were jack pines when we built our house. They were a lot better than no trees. I gradually cut them down and replaced them with white and red pines and spruce because jacks are usually not long-lived, and we planned to stay a while.

Many areas have fewer jack pines than they once did. Some were cut to make way for irrigated agriculture and others have fallen victim to forest succession and bud worm. Nothing stays the same in a woodland.

Poison Plants

If you had toxic plants growing on your property, what would you do? We have, or had, at least four species and we haven't done much because we don't think we have to.

One species is poison ivy. I made a half-hearted effort to eradicate it, but there's probably still some in the yard. One thing I did was show the kids how to recognize it and stay away from it. Poison ivy produces berries that birds eat without ill effects, but I don't recommend that you eat them.

I believe the stinging nettle we once had has disappeared. It's a plant you don't want to brush up against because it causes an annoying irritation if it touches bare skin. But unlike a poison ivy rash, it doesn't last long.

What about deadly nightshade? Its name is something of a misnomer. At least one source says you don't want to eat its berries, but if for some reason you do, you might get sick but you will survive. We don't eat them.

Rounding out the list of poisonous plants in our yard is white snakeroot. This one can be a killer but only in very limited circumstances. The problem with snakeroot is that when cows eat it, their milk may be poisonous.

But snakeroot grows in the woods and farmers nowadays seldom pasture their dairy cattle there. And if they do, the milk gets so diluted with other milk at the dairy plant that it's not noticeable. That wasn't true many years ago. Milk poisoned by snakeroot is said to have killed Abraham Lincoln's mother.

We haven't tried to eradicate the snakeroot on our property because we don't keep cows in our yard.

The Grass Killer

No grass grows outside our living room window. It used to, but another plant killed it. The killer was wild sarsaparilla.

Wild sarsaparilla grows 12 to 18 inches high and its leaves cast a dense shade, making it impossible for grass to grow underneath.

I could probably kill the invader, but why? Less grass means less lawn to mow, and the sarsaparilla is kind of attractive.

Its blossoms aren't in a class with azaleas and roses, and they're beneath the leaves where you can hardly see them. Still, the foliage is nice and green and when it dies in fall, it shrivels up and there's hardly anything to rake.

I didn't plant the sarsaparilla, at least not deliberately. I believe it came with a young pine tree I moved in from the woods, and it spread. It's a forest understory plant and is related to ginseng, but unlike ginseng, has no commercial value.

True sarsaparilla is a tropical plant that can be made into a soft drink. I guess you can make a substitute out of the wild sarsaparilla's roots, but I haven't tried.

Its cousin, ginseng, also grows wild. It's farmed too, with the Wausau area a hotbed for commercial production. Because it doesn't thrive under direct sunlight, ginseng is grown under plastic or wood slats which provide partial shade, as in a forest.

A lot of the ginseng grown in Wisconsin is exported to China, where people believe it's an aphrodisiac and a heart stimulant. The word ginseng, in fact, is of Chinese origin. Western scientists question ginseng's stimulant and aphrodisiac effects, but if you think a medicine helps, it probably does. You know, the placebo effect.

Prolific Pollinator

Pines pollinate prolifically. If you live in or near a pine woods, you know what I mean.

Years ago, I was at a meeting where a woman said her yard had been sprayed with pesticides, probably by a crop duster. Maybe it had been. I wasn't there. But she said she lived among pine trees, leading me to suspect that the dust she saw was pollen.

We live among pine trees and when the pollen is really thick and the wind is blowing, it's as if a yellow cloud is drifting through our yard. It's not a serious problem (we're not allergic to it), but it makes it hard to keep the house dust-free.

The different pine species aren't courteous enough to pollinate all at once and get it over with. First the jack pines pollinate, then the reds (Norways), and finally the whites. We have all three species in our neighborhood, so we get a good long dusting.

The pollen, of course, is essential for the reproduction of the pines. The pollen volume seems to vary from year to year, and so does the production of pine cones. One year a huge number of cones developed on our white pines. When they fell, I couldn't just pick them up off the driveway, I had to use a push broom.

Before falling, the cones released their seeds, and the following spring hundreds of little white pines sprouted in our yard.

Few of them survived. They never do. Nature produces a surplus of offspring as insurance.

Karner Blue Butterfly

ODDS AND ENDS

The Wisconsin Dog

Its proper name is American water spaniel, but you might call it the Wisconsin dog. It was developed here, and a rural Plainfield man, Paul Bovee, was sure he saved it from extinction. At one time, he believed he was the only one breeding the dog.

The American water spaniel is probably a mix of the Irish water spaniel, the now extinct English water spaniel, the curly-coated retriever, and maybe other breeds. A New London, Wisconsin man, Dr. Fred Pfeiffer, is credited with standardizing the dog so it breeds true.

It's a hunting dog, developed for retrieving waterfowl, but smaller than a Labrador or Chesapeake. It's also used for flushing and retrieving upland game like ruffed grouse.

It's a pretty good house dog, too. It's not like those hulking breeds that swish their tails and knock the porcelain off the coffee table.

Is it pretty? No offense intended, but for looks it doesn't match breeds like the Irish setter, with its glorious chestnut coat. American water spaniels are brown and sort of drab. That's not so bad. If it was pretty, breeders would try to make it even prettier. That's been the downfall of the Irish setter, one of those dogs that have been bred for their looks without concern for intelligence or health.

Some Irish setters, it's said, get lost at the end of a leash. The

English bulldog is an example of a breed with numerous health problems caused by bad breeding practices. Bovee sold a lot of dogs, but he said he wasn't running a puppy mill.

Why is the American water spaniel not better known? Bovee thought one reason was its name. "Water spaniel" conjures up the image of a wet dog, one that would mess up your davenport if you let it in the house.

But Bovee said it makes a good pet. Friendly, but not inclined to aggravate the neighbors by barking at the moon all night. Of course the animal gets damp retrieving ducks, but even then, said Bovee, it doesn't have a wet dog smell.

One of Bovee's buyers was a Saudi Arabian man. Where's a water dog going to swim in that bone-dry country? The customer told him he had a two-acre swimming pool despite the fact that he'd lucklessly drilled for water many times. "All he ever hit was that darned crude," said Bovee.

Only a few recognized dog breeds have ever been developed in the United States and the American water spaniel is the only one created in Wisconsin. It's the official state dog.

Butterflies

Everyone's familiar with the monarch, the big butterfly with the orange and black wings. It's an insect that depends on a specific plant for its survival, and so does the Karner blue butterfly.

The Karner blue can't move mountains, but it might force an adjustment in highway construction plans. It's federally endangered, and its principal stronghold is in Wisconsin.

This little insect, about thumbnail-size as an adult, depends on the wild lupine plant, since that's all its larvae eat. If there's a plot of lupines with Karner blues in it, and there's a plan to run a road through it, the road may have to move.

What's so special about this insect? It has no commercial value, but it's scarce, part of our native fauna, and deserves to survive.

Karner blue eggs hatch in spring, and after they turn into adults, they lay eggs. The second butterfly generation lays more eggs, and these are the ones that overwinter, hatching the following spring.

If you're a butterfly collector, forget the Karner blue. You can't collect it without a permit from the U.S. Fish & Wildlife Service.

The butterfly is named for a city in New York State. The man who named it was Vladimir Nabokov, a Russian-born novelist who wrote *Lolita*. He was also a lepidopterist, a butterfly and moth specialist.

Odds and Ends

The monarch butterfly is far more common than the Karner blue and has an even more interesting lifestyle. The plant it depends on is the milkweed and its relatives, such as the butterfly weed, a plant with gorgeous orange blossoms that grows wild around here. The monarch's larvae feed only on members of the milkweed family.

West of the Rocky Mountains, monarchs winter along the California coast. Here they go south to a mountainous area in Mexico, a migration of well over a thousand miles. The altitude is high and the air is cool, and the butterflies semi-hibernate.

Toward spring, the monarchs come alive and head north. They die along the way, but not before laying eggs. The eggs hatch and the insects continue their journey. A few generations after leaving Mexico, they're in the north. The following fall, several generations later, they start back to Mexico.

For a long time, the monarchs' wintering site was a mystery. It was located through returns of bands. How do you band a butterfly? Not like you band a bird. In the case of the insects, little adhesive patches are placed on the wings.

Clamming

The headline on July 31, 1918, called clamming "Stevens Point's leading industry." It was no doubt tongue-in-cheek, but nevertheless harvesting clams or mussels from the Wisconsin River was a big business in its day.

The story under the headline said clamshell buyer Lon Myers estimated $100,000 had been paid to clammers in the Stevens Point area in recent months. The price for shells ranged from $45 to $53 a ton, so $100,000 translates to about 2,000 tons.

One local clammer was Dave Field, whose profits helped pay off the mortgage on Treasure Island near Plover, where the family farmed.

The shells were used in button manufacture. An Iowa company, Kautz & Irvine, had a factory on the Wisconsin River in Stevens Point at Wells Point, a present-day marina. There it punched out blanks from the shells and sent them elsewhere for finishing, usually to Muscatine and other places in Iowa.

In shallow water, clams could be picked off the river bottom by hand and tossed in a boat. In deeper water, the clammers used drags—chains with blunt hooks attached which were pulled across the bottom by a boat. The clams closed their shells on the hooks and were hauled in.

On shore, the clams were put in hot water to kill them and the meat was removed. In the process, it was examined for pearls. Once in a while, one was found but it was rarely valuable.

Local commercial clamming apparently ended in the late 1920s. By then, clams were probably getting scarce because of overharvesting and water pollution.

Clamming continued elsewhere and many of the shells went to Japan. There the pieces were inserted in oysters, which secreted a substance that coated them and turned them into cultured pearls.

Another reason for the reduction in clam populations was the damming of rivers. Some species require swift water, and dams slow the flow. Still another reason was the disappearance of certain fish species. Many clams go through a stage where their larvae have to attach to a fish.

The skipjack herring is the primary host for the larvae of the ebony shell clam. With the disappearance from Wisconsin waters of the skipjack herring, the ebony shell clam seems to have vanished too.

Today, commercial clamming is illegal in Wisconsin. People aren't allowed to take a live clam, or even the shell of a dead one if it's from one of the state's many threatened or endangered clam species.

Creepy, Crawly Critters

Count yourself among the great majority if you dislike snakes. But did you ever ask yourself why?

Maybe you were warned when you were a kid that they're poisonous, though most of them aren't. Or maybe it's instinct. I'm told apes, our cousins, fear snakes and I'm sure no one told them they were toxic. So maybe it's in our genes.

It's extremely unlikely you'll ever encounter a poisonous snake in Wisconsin outside of the southwest part. And not very likely there either.

A man once told me one reason he liked it here was that he didn't have to look down on the ground all the time—meaning there was no need to worry about poisonous snakes. He said there were "suspicious accounts" of venomous snakes here, but they weren't authenticated. In other words, just possibly there was, or had been, a poisonous snake or two in the vicinity, but it was unproven.

Wisconsin has only two venomous snake species, the massasauga, or swamp rattlesnake, and the timber rattler. The massasauga is small and doesn't carry much venom, and a healthy adult probably wouldn't be seriously harmed if bitten. The timber rattler is more dangerous, but there's no recent record of one biting anyone fatally in Wisconsin.

Odds and Ends

What about water moccasins? They're poisonous and sometimes people say they've seen them here. What they probably saw were non-toxic water snakes, not moccasins, which aren't found any closer to Wisconsin than Southern Illinois.

We have numerous non-venomous snake species here. They aren't hurting anyone and are doing us some good by controlling small rodents. But people sometimes kill these harmless critters without thinking.

Wisconsin's non-venomous snakes, as listed by the Department of Natural Resources, are as listed:

    prairie ringneck snake
    northern ringneck snake
    eastern hognose snake
    smooth green snake
    yellow-bellied (blue racer) snake
    black rat (pilot) snake
    western fox (pine) snake
    bull snake
    eastern milk snake
    Butler's garter snake
    eastern plains garter snake
    northern ribbon snake
    western ribbon snake
    common garter snake
    brown (DeKay's) snake
    northern redbelly snake
    queen snake
    northern water snake

The massasauga, western ribbon, northern ribbon, and queen are endangered, the yellow-bellied (blue racer), black rat, bull, and timber rattler are protected, Butler's is threatened, and the northern ringneck and prairie ringneck snakes are species of special concern.

The pine snake is sometimes mistaken for a copperhead snake (not found in Wisconsin) or a rattlesnake. The yellow-bellied or blue racer, found in the western part of the state, is among North America's fastest snakes, zipping along at speeds up to four miles an hour.

Despite Eve's unfortunate experience in the Garden of Eden, we should be adopting a live and let live attitude toward snakes, meanwhile keeping our distance from the rattlers.

Snoop and Scoop

Snoop was a Dalmatian, but not a high-class one. She had the required number of spots, but somehow didn't measure up to the standards of the breed, sometimes called the coach dog. They wouldn't have let her in the back door at the Westminster Kennel Club. She apparently wasn't a purebred, but then neither am I.

Dalmatians aren't a hunting breed, but sometimes you come across a throwback, and I got to thinking: maybe there was a pointing dog in Snoop's ancestry. I tested her on a ruffed grouse hunting trip in the Dewey Marsh State Wildlife Area.

A good grouse dog ranges ahead of you, but not too far. If it flushes a bird beyond shotgun range, it's worse than having no dog at all. We walked along a forest trail with Snoop in the lead, but not too far in front. Then a grouse flushed and I shot.

After that, Snoop was no longer in front of me. She was behind me, maybe 40 feet back. When I walked, Snoop walked, and when I stopped, Snoop stopped, still 40 feet in the rear. Snoop was gun-shy, a trait I believe is incurable.

I never took Snoop hunting again but she remained a fine family pet for the rest of her life, which lasted almost 15 years.

Before Snoop, I had a dog named Scoop. He was a nice dog,

though he had a weak stomach and was somewhat gassy. Scoop was a Boston terrier, definitely not a hunting breed.

He had a grudge against wildlife, and among the creatures he didn't like were little snakes, which he grabbed by the tail and shook. It was like cracking a whip and it was fatal to the snakes, which I regretted as they were non-poisonous and totally harmless.

Snoop also attacked a skunk on one occasion and a porcupine on another. The skunk odor bothered us more than it did him, but the same couldn't be said for the porcupine quills.

He was left with a face full of quills, none of which, fortunately, penetrated an eye. But he couldn't walk around looking like a pin cushion, so we tried to remove the quills with a pair of pliers. Scoop wouldn't stand still, so we put a rope around his neck and tightened it until he passed out. It was probably something we shouldn't have done, but it seemed to be an emergency. Anyway, it worked. He revived after the rope was removed. By that time we'd finished the quill-removal job, or so we thought.

A few days later we discovered we'd missed a quill in one of his hind legs. It worked its way in and came out the other side and Scoop was as good as new.

Did he learn a lesson? I doubt it. He wasn't real bright, and if he'd had the opportunity to attack another porcupine, I'm sure he'd have done it. But he never saw another one.

Homemade Fakes

If you use factory-made decoys and expertly tied flies, you may shoot more ducks and catch more trout than with homemade ones.

But it's more fun to use the ones you made yourself. And having fun is why we fish and hunt, isn't it?

My fly-tying skills are so limited that every one I've ever made was an original, even when I was trying to make it look like a Hornberg or a Blue Wing Olive.

It didn't always matter. The biggest fish I ever caught on one of my own flies was an 18-inch brown trout that hit on one of the worst lures I ever tied, a shapeless blob of deer hair. You may have caught bigger trout and so have I, but what made it memorable was that it hit on one of my own creations.

As for decoys, I only made scaups, which most duck hunters call bluebills. Maybe I should have made mallards, the most common ducks in the typical hunter's bag around here. But bluebills are easier to paint—just black and white with, of course, blue bills.

I carved most of them out of solid blocks of wood, but a few were of boards glued together with hollow interiors to make them lighter.

You learn as you go along, and I found that my decoys tipped over in the water on a windy day. I solved the problem with lead keel weights.

Did my homemade decoys attract ducks? I think they did but I'm not sure. Anyway, they didn't scare them away.

Fishing plugs are also fun to make. I've only made a few, and my most memorable catch using one was a decent-sized northern pike where Hay Meadow Creek joins the Wisconsin River. I wish I'd made more plugs, not to put more fish in the freezer, but just for the heck of it.

Lake or Dry Land?

Unscrupulous land agents used to sell rocky farms in winter when snow covered the ground and the buyer couldn't see the boulders.

Unscrupulous waterfront sellers peddled lakefront property to unwitting buyers in the years when lakes had water. Not all lakes are full all the time. In some of them, the water table fluctuates and so do lake levels. When they're high, that's the time to sell lots.

Irrigation and municipal wells can affect stream flows and lake levels. But even without pumping, water levels may go up and down, depending on the precipitation. In some lakes, the level doesn't vary much. In others, it may change only a foot or two. In still others, the change is dramatic. They dry up.

So if you wanted to cash in on a lake that sometimes disappeared, you had to do it when it had water.

One such lake is Boelter, in southeastern Portage County. An Appleton firm acquired it, subdivided the shoreline, and put the lots on the market. It was a year when the lake had water in it, though it wasn't full to the brim. You could tell that by an old water mark along the shore, a few feet above the current level. But it still looked fairly good.

The land company held a sort of outdoor open house for potential buyers. It advertised it heavily, saying, "It's wet—it's wooded—it's got a sandy beach—and it's pretty." A good crowd showed up and kept the company's salesmen busy. One of them told me the lake was 10 or 15 feet deep. I asked whether the level was constant, he said, "We don't think it will go down. Maybe a little."

In its printed material, the land company made no claims about the lake's depth or its constant level. It did, however, say panfishing was excellent. The salesman wasn't so sure. "We think it has panfish and bullheads," he said. "We haven't fished it ourselves."

"There were no zoning restrictions regulating building setbacks or architectural design," said the salesman.

The Department of Natural Resources publishes a booklet that lists the lakes in Wisconsin, county by county, but there's no mention of Boelter, its size, or its depth. Maybe the DNR gathered its material at a time when Boelter Lake had neither size nor depth because it was dry. That happens periodically.

On the day the land company was holding its outdoor open house, people living in the area who knew the lake said they doubted it was more than six or eight feet deep. A few years earlier, one man said, "You had trouble getting your feet wet when you walked across it."

Subsequently the lake level went up, then it went down. It always did and always will.

The land company may have done Portage County one favor. A county zoning ordinance was adopted, probably at least in part because of the company's tactics, and it contains restrictions not in effect at the time of the Boelter Lake lot scam.

Mound Builders

Indian mounds are evidence that the first people in Wisconsin weren't French voyageurs. Even the mound builders were latecomers. Other people were here when glacial ice still lingered, 10,000 or more years ago.

But the mound builders are the ones who left the most evidence. Many of the mounds are burial sites. Others are effigies, often in the shape of animals and people, and they may have had a religious significance or were clan symbols.

In the 19th century, people trying to explain the mounds' origin came up with all kinds of crazy theories. They said the mounds had been built by a lost race, or Vikings, or Greeks, or Welshmen. Or, of course, the lost tribes of Israel. But all the evidence points to American Indians as the builders.

A few mounds were in the form of flat-topped temple platforms, the most impressive of which is at Cahokia, Illinois, covering 16 acres. It was built by people who had no earth-moving equipment. It's made up of 22 million cubic feet of soil and its base is almost 1,000 feet long on each side. Aztalan State Park, in Southern Wisconsin, also has platform mounds, but not that big.

Many of Wisconsin's mounds have been ruined by the plow

or urban sprawl. In Portage County, some remain in Lake Emily Park, Whiting Village Park, and on private land. They're protected by law now, but they weren't always. A fine collection, the Bigelow Mounds, lay along the Wisconsin River in Plover. I was there when one of the mounds was excavated years ago. At the bottom was the skeleton of a woman. Unfortunately, the Bigelow mounds weren't protected. They're now the site of a residential subdivision.

Portage County also has what appears to be an Indian ceremonial ring. It was mentioned in the October 1913 issue of *The Wisconsin Archeologist*. Some years ago, our son Jim and I went hunting for it. It's in the eastern part of the county, close to a couple of lakes. The landowner gave us permission to look for it but said we probably wouldn't recognize it because his cows had trampled it flat.

But they hadn't. The ring was obvious. It was a raised circle of earth and had clearly been there long time, as good-sized trees were growing out of it. Artifacts like this are worth preserving.

Changing Rules

Pete Peters of Stevens Point, a storehouse of information on things related to the outdoors, once showed me a copy of the 1925 Wisconsin fishing and hunting regulations. Things were less complicated in those days (what wasn't?) and all the rules were in one small pamphlet.

Many fish species went by different names back then. No mention was made of bluegills and sunfish, but calico bass and strawberry bass were listed. Maybe bluegills and sunfish went by other names?

Northern pike were called pickerels, a name now usually reserved for a smaller member of the pike family found in Southern Wisconsin. Pike were listed, but they were what we now call walleyes.

The largemouth bass was mentioned along with an alternate name, Oswego green, and an alternate name for the smallmouth was yellow bass.

Deer weren't plentiful when the pamphlet was published. In the 1920s, many counties didn't have a deer season and in those that did, it was bucks-only and often it was open only every other year.

Waterfowl hunters were allowed a whopping 15 ducks a day, but no wood ducks. You could use up to five live duck decoys.

Prairie chickens were still legal game in some counties, but

197

the season lasted only four days. So did the ruffed grouse season. Pheasant hunting was closed statewide.

In 1925, you could shoot all the wolves you wanted. The same with lynx, bobcats, gray foxes, badgers, woodchucks, red squirrels, great horned owls, snowy owls, kingfishers, and several kinds of hawks. And you could do it year around.

Great blue herons were protected only near their rookeries.

Those were the good old days, but not always too good.

A Hard Water Business

Before the arrival of the refrigerator, just about every city in Wisconsin had an ice business. Ice was cut on lakes and rivers and stored in ice houses. Often sawdust was packed around it for insulation so it wouldn't all melt in summer.

A lot of work was involved in cutting the ice, lifting it out of the water, hauling it to the ice houses, and then delivering it to homes and businesses. Sometimes farm families cut their own, using hand-powered saws, but the commercial cutters eventually mechanized their operations.

For years, horse-drawn wagons hauled ice to the customers. Burly men wearing rubber capes hoisted the blocks onto their shoulders with tongs and carried them in. They put them in ice boxes, forerunners of refrigerators. The ice boxes had a drain pipe, and as the blocks melted, the water ran into the basement, generally onto a dirt floor.

Kids used to follow the wagons and grab slivers of ice to suck on hot summer days. They were taking a chance because often the ice was cut on polluted waters, and a lot of germs survive freezing.

Residential ice deliveries persisted until after World War II. In Stevens Point, the ice business lasted until 1972 because the Soo Line Railroad continued using it in its refrigerator cars, storing it in big insulated buildings near the tracks.

Casey Distributing Co. of Stevens Point was probably the last commercial ice harvester in Wisconsin, making its final cut on McDill Pond. A lot of the earlier harvesting was on the Wisconsin River.

Pat Casey, who headed the company, said cutting usually began when the ice was about 16 inches thick. In a cold winter, it might be 33 inches thick at the end of the harvest, and a block weighed about 650 pounds. But Casey said it skidded pretty well.

Fracking Sand

Mineral resources are a blessing. We all use stuff that comes from mines. But sometimes there's a downside, like the effects of mining on the terrain and on streams and lakes. This is even true of fracking sand mines.

No one had heard of fracking sand until companies looking for oil and natural gas started using hydraulic fracturing (hence fracking) to crack rock formations. This entails pumping water underground under high pressure, along with certain chemicals and sand. The purpose of the sand is to keep the cracks open. And not just any old sand. Fracking sand granules are rounded so oil and gas can seep through.

No hydraulic fracturing is occurring in Wisconsin because it doesn't have petroleum as far as anyone knows, but the western part of the state has lots of fracking sand. It's different from the sand deposited by glacial outwash.

Portage County, where I live, doesn't have fracking sand. That's bad news if you want to make a killing selling your land to a sand mining company. Good news if you want to avoid the controversies that have come with sand mining in other counties.

Opponents of fracking sand mining say it might threaten groundwater, and that windblown particles of the fine sand could cause lung problems. And there's concern about trucks carrying heavy sand loads damaging roads.

Big money is being paid for land that has fracking sand, and for the sand itself. The average well in Pennsylvania is said to use about 5,000,000 pounds, or 2,500 tons. At $200 a ton, the going price at one point, that's a half-million dollars worth of sand.

Bruce Brown, senior geologist with the Wisconsin Geological Survey, said there's plenty of sand in Portage County, but it's not the right kind for fracking. "Most of it is glacial outwash sand, and sand along the Wisconsin River," he said. It's too angular, meaning the grains aren't rounded. Also it contains many impurities.

In Western Wisconsin, much of the sand is derived from the local bedrock and is suitable for fracking. Glacial outwash sand is "great for aggregate used in concrete and asphalt, and may be, in some cases, suitable for foundry sand, but it will not meet the tight purity and roundness specs for frack sand," Brown said.

If Portage County wanted to cash in on the boom, "I'm afraid you are likely out of luck," Brown said. "If on the other hand you wanted to avoid the issues making news in ... the western counties, you are in luck."

The state of Wisconsin has no regulations for mining fracking sand, other than those covering other types of sand mining, but local units of government have some control. They can deny permission for a pit or approve it with conditions, such as the slope of the excavation, hours of operation, and what needs to be done to reclaim the site after excavation ends.

Conclusion

I was at the Naval Air Museum in Pensacola, Florida, and saw an IMAX film about the Hubble space telescope. Hubble, you may recall, was put into orbit to peer into the depths of the universe and it equaled, or maybe exceeded, expectations. There's a lot to see out there—millions and billions of stars. Or is it trillions and quadrillions?

Whichever, it's mind-bending and makes you feel insignificant. Our planet is just a speck of dust in the cosmos, but it's our speck, the only one we have, and we should be taking care of it.

As I said in the introduction, this book wasn't intended to be a "me and Joe went fishin'" saga, though I wish Joe well and hope he catches his limit. (But please, Joe, release at least some of what you catch.)

Mostly, I hope it alerts people to the need to protect our environment, including air, water, and soil. We, as a people, haven't been doing that very well, though we seem to be getting a little better.

Some of our lawmakers, when presented with a choice between hyping the economy in the short run and protecting the environment in the long run, will go after the fast buck. Of course jobs are important, but if something like a mine creates jobs while causing catastrophic environmental damage, wouldn't it be good to take the long view and at least not let the miners write the mining laws? Mines aren't here forever. The land is.

We have an obligation to be good stewards of the Earth. So flick off the lights when you leave the room. It's not the answer to the world's energy problems, but you have to start somewhere.

Sorry for the sermon. I hope you enjoyed the book.

Selected Bibliography

This bibliography contains selected works and sources significant to the writing of this book. It is intended to serve as a reference to those who wish to read more about the ideas presented within.

Becker, George C. *Fishes of Wisconsin*. Madison: University of Wisconsin Press, 1983.

Hacker, Vern. *A Fine Kettle of Fish*. Madison: Wisconsin Dept. of Natural Resources, 1977.

Hamerstrom, Frances. *Strictly for the Chickens*. Ames: Iowa State Univ. Press, 1980.

Hamerstrom, Frances. *Is She Coming Too?* Ames: Iowa State Univ. Press, 1989.

Jackson, Hartley H.T. *Mammals of Wisconsin*. Madison: University of Wisconsin Press, 1961.

Krug, Merton E. *DuBay: Son-In-Law of Oshkosh*. Appleton: C.C. Nelson, 1946.

Long, Charles A. *The Wild Mammals of Wisconsin*. Sofia: Pensoft, 2008.

Menzel, Roy. *Every Heart Harbors a Hometown on the River*. Stevens Point: Journal Printing Company and Palmer Productions, 1989.

Meyer, G.J. *A World Undone: The Story of the Great War, 1914-1918*. New York: Delacorte Press, 2006.

Rosholt, Malcolm Leviatt. *Pioneers of the Pinery*. Rosholt: Rosholt House, 1979.

Cornerstone Press Staff

Chief Executive Officer	Dan Dieterich
President	Dylan Croft
Editor-in-Chief	Eric Schreiber
Substance Editor	Emily Alger-Feser
Associate Substance Editors	Lisa Deakins
	Billy Klassen
	Randy Ploeckelman
Copy Editor	Connor Falk
Associate Copy Editors	Erich Maas
	Rachel Pukall
	Jillian Phillips
Production Director	Vanessa L. Gribowski
Lead Designer	Sara Rebers
Design Associate	Rebecca Finger
Director of Marketing	Kea Gregorich
Advertising Manager	Cassie Scott
Advertising Associate	Emily Johnson
Publicity Manager	Aaron Krish
Publicity Associate	Hilary Neesam
Social Media Manager	Lauren Nelsen
Social Media Associate	Stephanie School
Director of Sales	Rebecca A. Whitehead
Business Manager	Justin Lindberg
Fulfillment Manager	Brittany Waite